Letters to Growing Pastors

Letters to Growing Pastors

Reflections on Ministry for Coffee-Cup Conversations

Howard D. Vanderwell

Foreword by
Jul Medenblik

WIPF & STOCK · Eugene, Oregon

LETTERS TO GROWING PASTORS
Reflections on Ministry for Coffee-Cup Conversations

Wipf & Stock
An Imprint of Wipf and Stock Publishers
199 W. 8th Ave., Suite 3
Eugene, OR 97401

www.wipfandstock.com

PAPERBACK ISBN: 978-1-5326-4080-3
HARDCOVER ISBN: 978-1-5326-4081-0
EBOOK ISBN: 978-1-5326-4082-7

Manufactured in the U.S.A.

All Scripture quotations are taken from the Holy Bible
New International Version NIV
Copyright 1978, New York International Bible Society

To Ellie

My lifelong suitable helper,

Who has served by my side in ministry

And has supported me while I have had to work through

All these issues.

Your help has been invaluable.

Contents

CONTENTS

Foreword

I FIRST MET REV. Howard Vanderwell in 1990 as he took up the position of president at the annual, bi-national (US and Canada) general assembly of pastors and church leaders for the denomination that we both serve. Howie had been voted into his position by those who were delegates to the assembly. I did not know Rev. Vanderwell, but over the next two weeks I came to know through his words and actions that the delegates had been right in their selection.

Before me stood a pastor who was honest, hopeful and deeply in love with the church. The church in that moment was in deep conflict and division. He stood at the center and with gentle humor and deep devotion, he pastored and led. I never forgot his work then and I am privileged to now count Howie as a colleague, mentor and friend.

You may not be able to physically sit down and talk to Howie and hear his wisdom, insights and encouragement, but this book is the next best thing. He has written this book with you in mind.

In twenty-one concise chapters, you will find a tapestry that combines spiritual memoir, testimony, thoughtful reflections and key questions no matter how long you have been a pastor. Howie's own ministry was marked by his desire to grow as a pastor. His reflections and probing of not only his own journey, but also his invitation for you to join the journey comes from a heart that has been captured and formed by the grace of God.

I have had many mentors in life. This book is written by a mentor who has lived where you now live and who, despite the difficult times in ministry, continued to model along with his wonderful wife, Ellie, grace, humility, joy and servanthood.

Rev. Howard Vanderwell is a leader in the church of Jesus Christ. He never fully retired because he continued to pastor. Through teaching, conferences and many articles and books (like this one), he has continued to lift up the proven promises of God. May you enjoy "sharing a cup of coffee" or other beverage with someone you will come to know as a colleague, mentor and friend.

Thank you, Howie, for the letters you have written to us!

Rev. Jul Medenblik
President of Calvin Theological Seminary

Five Formative Comments

SOMETIMES A SIMPLE COMMENT has great power to form us. Great formative influences can be wrapped up in a small statement that might easily escape notice. I'm conscious of five such statements which may not have seemed so big when they were originally spoken, but have proved to be greatly influential in my life. I cite these to prompt you to look for such gifts others have given you.

You are a baptized boy!

These are my father's words. They were spoken often, usually quite directly. And as I recall they were often spoken to me when I was on the verge of or had already engaged in some foolish behavior. "Remember, Howard, you are a baptized boy," are words that were intended to take me back to a baptism Sunday in 1937 in Muskegon, Michigan, when my parents presented me for baptism and God placed his claim on me. The pastor happened to be my grandfather. "I baptize you in the name of the Father, the Son, and the Holy Spirit," he said as the drops of water trickled down my forehead. It was a solemn moment in which I received my identity as a child of God. God had claimed me as his own, his covenant child, and I was always to consider this a profound privilege. But I was also to sense the challenge in those words for God had spoken of his claim on my life and his claim was to move me to a life of total obedience as a child of God. To this day I hear those formative words ringing in my ears. I hope you hear similar words.

Many others would love to be where you are!

I heard these words in the sanctuary of the Lebanon Church in Sioux Center, Iowa. It was 1962, a Friday evening ordination service when I entered the Christian ministry. I was relieved to be at this point, knowing that my seminary education and the qualifying exams were all behind me. I was excited, anticipating all the joys and rigors of the ministry. My uncle, Rev. Peter Eldersveld, was preaching at my ordination service and in his charge to me he was very direct. "Howard," he said looking straight at me, "you stand in a privileged spot . . . many others would love to be where you are!" He meant that being a minister of the gospel was a high and holy calling, and he also meant that being a minister in a church that stands firmly on the Word of God is the best place to be. I came back to those words often.

You will find the ministry to be this busy and more!

Once I began the journey of my ministry I remembered these words that I had heard in seminary. They were spoken by Dr. John Kromminga, the president of Calvin Theological Seminary, while I was a student there. Our class had become very critical of the seminary curriculum, believing that the demands were just too many and the work load was unreasonably heavy. We were convinced some of the professors were overly demanding, and we requested a meeting with the president to air some of our grievances. We expected him to be somewhat sympathetic to our concerns. He listened carefully, and then surprised us by his response. "If you think you are busy now, just wait until you are in the ministry. You'll find the ministry to be this busy and more." He unapologetically warned us that the struggle with too many assignments would not end once we left seminary. Instead it would likely increase. We were disappointed, but later during our ministries his comments made a lot of sense. I remembered that there seemed to be too many tasks in the pastorate to balance all at once. Dr. Kromminga's words then became a call to time management, prioritizing, and self-discipline. All of it hard work!

You are not ready until you have laid between the two white sheets!

This comment came in a letter and it surprised me. Two months after my ordination to the ministry I was hospitalized with a hemorrhaging ulcer. I was very distressed, to say the least, and was asking some very hard questions about why this should happen and why it should happen now. One of those questions was, "Does this mean I can't handle the ministry?" My parents heard of my distress, and apparently wrote a relative of mine, a fellow pastor, who wrote me this letter with such timely advice—"You are not ready to care for others until you have laid between the two white sheets yourself." It jolted me into realizing that a hospital bed was an extension of the classroom. This new awareness taught me to look at this event as continued formation for ministry, not an interruption in ministry. Little did I know how much of my ministry would be involved with folks who are suffering, and as the years rolled on I looked back on this advice and learned to see it as God's hand in giving me a new perspective and shaping me with a pastor's heart.

Just go out there and love them.

This one often came from my wife, though we had originally heard it from a senior colleague. The comment came often, and it usually came on Saturday night or Sunday morning while I was making my final preparations for preaching. I loved preaching, but there were many times when I was intimidated by it. Perhaps I just didn't feel ready, or I was too weary, or frustrated, or I felt a time of conflict and division brewing in the congregation. Any of those factors were able to erode my eagerness to stand before the congregation and lead them. She knew of my hesitancy and this was her advice, often repeated just before church time. "Just go out there and love them." It reminded me of what was most important after all.

Any one of these five people, and their five comments, might well have been long forgotten. But God shapes us strategically by people and their comments in often unexpected ways. The more I recalled these five, the more conscious I became of all the little ways he leads through others with little comments that can too easily be overlooked.

How many similar comments can you recall?

"Grow where you planted"
                                Betty Holland
"Always speak from your heart
God works best through you
that way"
                        Jean Sandbach
                        Mark Allen

Preface

I AM IMAGINING A few of us leisurely chatting over a cup of coffee. We've just spent two days at a preaching conference. It's been a good conference for us with many new ideas. Now we have a bit of free time before the closing worship service this evening, so we decided to meet in the coffee shop.

Most of us knew each other as classmates in seminary some years ago and it felt good to spend some time reconnecting, reminiscing about our experiences in seminary, and musing on the expectations we carried into our ministries. Gradually we became more vulnerable with each other and were willing to admit that though we find our ministries rewarding and challenging, we're also surprised at how weary we become, how frequently disillusionment knocks at our door, and how surprised we are at the big questions that come up. We've each been in our ministries from five to seven years, and we're beginning to wonder if that isn't a risky passage we have to go through on the way to the rest of our ministry.

I write these words for pastors like you and others, perhaps less than ten years out of seminary, and now serving with a mixture of excitement and satisfaction on the one hand, and weariness and uncertainty on the other.

I write to you out of my own experiences, with an eagerness to give you hope and encouragement. I've spent a lifetime in the pastorate, four congregations over forty years. On the one hand it's been a wonderful journey, but it has also wearied me and at times has puzzled me. After forty years I retired from the pastorate and now I have the time and leisure to look at the ministry objectively, sorting it all out in a way I wasn't able to do while busily immersed in it. Sometimes we can see things more clearly when we look at them through a rearview mirror.

Perhaps you will be able to sense in these pages that there are two things going on simultaneously—my efforts to objectively sort out and make sense of all that happens in this wonderful yet tantalizing life we call the life of the pastor, and also my attempt to find ways in which I convey to you the kind of insights that will help you along. I hope that putting something of myself and my ministry into print will give you encouragement, direction and understanding. For too many of us our stories end when our ministry or our life ends. When the stories end they are easily lost forever and no one will learn from them anymore. How sad! And how much better to capture and record our stories for the sake of those who follow us. So I write about my story in the hope that you will better understand your own story and that the traces of God's hand in your ministry will become more apparent.

During my life as a pastor, I have been helped immeasurably by several pastors, much older than I, who took the time and effort when I was a young pastor to open their hearts and experiences to me so I could learn from them and grow. If, along the way, I am able to encourage others like yourself to join your reflections with mine, we'll all find it more satisfying.

However, I think there is another motive behind my writing of these words. I am convinced that writing can be an act of gratitude. I have had a wonderful life, filled with powerful blessings, and more opportunities for good wide-ranging service than I ever expected. So I intend that this act of writing about it all and opening it up to you is an act of deep gratitude to God who made it all possible. I stand now near the end of my ministry years. The best years of my ministry are behind me, and who knows how many more good years I will have. I hope there will be many, but none of us knows. In any case, my desire is to stir deeply within you the awareness that you are serving in a high and holy calling that rightly requires your best, but will also tax you thoroughly. My aim, in light of that, is to encourage you to not to lose heart. Perhaps through my reflections I can serve those of you who are active in Christian ministry today.

You will find that these reflections arrange themselves around a number of defined topics that will become clear along the way. I'll tell you about my origins, my journey, and my calling. I'll also turn my attention to key people whom God has brought into my life and ministry to shape me in strategic ways. Most of these people would probably be surprised to find themselves here, yet God used them in unexpected ways to shape me and I'm grateful for each of them. I'll be thinking and talking about the life of the church. After all, the church has been the center of nearly my entire life, and I've seen the internal life of the church more thoroughly than most. There's inspiration in that . . . and also sadness. And like the church, the Christian ministry involves both inspiration as we work with God's Spirit and sadness when we are exposed to the underbelly of the church. And closely associated with that will be my reflection on the Christian ministry. I'm delighted that my whole life has been a life of ministry, even now in my retirement. Through the years, I've learned much about ministry that I wish I had known when I began. (But then, maybe not!) And I'll also take you into my own heart and some of the struggles that have gone on there. I don't know if others tend to struggle with big questions as much as I have, or maybe I'm just more willing to be candid about them. But while I've preached and taught and counseled and lived, I have been accompanied by some big internal issues of life and faith and I suppose in many respects they will never quite fully be resolved in this life. Surely all of these topics also find their way into your experiences. So I'll not hesitate to talk with you about such matters as God's mysteries, the testy demands of the ministry, questions, struggles, surprises, some disappointments, the cost, and the pain.

I have in mind particularly those of you who are less than ten years into your ministries because those early years are the ones in which some of the big questions come up for the first time, the trajectory of growth is rapid, and so is the experience of frustration and struggle. And those are the years when we are surprised to face things we never expected to encounter. I remember so clearly those early years of being a "young pastor" and my heart was so filled with both excitement and anxiety. I was thrilled to be a servant of Christ, but soon I began to understand Paul's comment about the fact that "we have this treasure in jars of clay" (2 Cor 4:7). Nearly all young pastors deal with a basketful of post-seminary questions—about themselves, their task, their resources, and their limitations. And they are confronted with the intense joy of ministry and the baffling struggles of it. And even more pressing is the underlying question of how clear my awareness is of the underlying movement of God in my own life.

Because these are written as letters, I envision us continuing on in that coffee shop while we keep on reflecting together. So pour yourself another cup of coffee and let's keep on talking about our ministries. I'll dig into my own awareness and experiences and I hope you will interact with me on the ideas that come up.

1

The Journey of an Ordinary Man

DEAR PASTOR,

It's probably best to start right at the beginning of my journey, which means April 8, 1937, in Muskegon, Michigan. I won't belabor all the details of my personal life, but I think you need to know enough of it to better understand much of what follows.

If, for some reason, your mind occasionally asks the question, "So just what kind of a person does God use in his ministry?" then I'll answer that with my story as a way of saying, "God most often uses common, ordinary people." Jesus himself was marked by an earthly life that was simple and unpretentious, with roots in out-of-the-way Nazareth. The disciples he chose were viewed as "unschooled and ordinary men" in Acts 4:13. And Paul specifically points to the Corinthian church as particularly ordinary people, which seems to be a mark of God's people.

In words that have always been particularly important to me, Paul says, "Not many of you were wise by human standards; not many were influential; not many were of noble birth. But God chose the foolish things of the world to shame the wise; God chose the weak things of the world to shame the strong. He chose the lowly things of this world and the despised things—and the things that are not—to nullify the things that are, so that no one may boast before him" (1 Cor 1:26–29).

1

My beginnings were rather inauspicious. I was born, apparently at home, to John and Kelly Vanderwell, who were at that time trying to recover from the setback of the Great Depression. I heard that they had lost a home during that time, though they never discussed that with us as their children. Now they were in this small comfortable home on Wood St. and aiming to begin their family. Russell was the first born. I was second, six years after him. Warren would come third, just five years later. My father had come here as an immigrant boy of eleven years old, with his family of ten siblings. Poverty, church, hard work, and very limited education were the themes of their family life.

I was baptized in First Church in Muskegon by my grandfather, Rev. Sietze (Samuel) Eldersveld, who was the pastor at the time. (My father married the preacher's daughter!) I must admit I don't have a lot of clear memories of my childhood, except that my two brothers and I all slept in the same bedroom upstairs— one double bed and one single bed. We seemed to get along well as brothers and I have no memories of tensions or fights, though I'm sure they must have happened—after all, we were boys and we were siblings.

Our family life was very even keeled and secure. Our all-important annual vacation times proved to be special memory-makers for us. Dad worked hard in the factory, Sealed Power Piston Rings, and I think he was determined that vacation time should make up for time lost as a family because of how hard he worked. I think also that the right to take a vacation was a symbol of the fact that they had arrived at a greater position of prosperity; they were "making it." Our customary vacation practice would be a week or two at a cottage in Lower Michigan—Silver Lake, Baptist Lake, Bear Lake, Carp Lake, etc. We always enjoyed the outside and leisure games together. But once in a while we'd take a trip. I remember when we travelled to Washington, DC, to learn history and Dad was thrilled that on the way back we got to travel on parts of the Pennsylvania Turnpike which was being built. At times we got on it and off it and back on it, as sections were completed—a whole new experience to be on a superhighway! Another year, we traveled to southwestern Minnesota to visit relatives. My brothers and I stayed on farms with "cousins" and I remember being so sad when it was time to pack up and head home. To us, Edgerton and Leota, Minnesota, were fascinating places.

All of my education took place in the Christian school system of Muskegon. My parents were deeply devoted to Christian education and served the school in many volunteer capacities. Grades 1–8 were in Muskegon Christian School, also called Hartford St. School, and grades 9–12 were in Western Michigan Christian High School. I enjoyed school, and did fairly well.

I worked all through high school at a local supermarket, first as a stock-boy and eventually as a butcher. (I enjoyed the latter so very much more.) I felt the dilemma, however, of being torn between two groups of "friends"—those in school and those at work. Those at work were not Christians and had a value system quite different from what I was taught. They often invited me to go with them after work, and I struggled hard with that, knowing it was not good company or influence for me. I know I wasn't always so pleasant for Mom and Dad at that stage. I could be quiet, uncooperative, and it gave them some concerns. While at work one day, my brother Russ stopped by and met me for coffee break. Quietly he asked me how I was, and he explained that Mom and Dad were worried about me and I should learn to be more responsive to them. I took that seriously. It was a wake-up call, and as I look back it was an act of healthy brother-love that he would confront me.

When college began, I came into my own. I had agreed to live with two classmates from high school. The three of us went to Grand Rapids to hunt for rooms to rent. It was very clear in our minds that we were launching out in life. We found what we wanted with Mrs. Hewitt on the corner of Giddings and Sherman St. We lived with her for a year, got along with her very well, and we even bought her car—a 1936 Ford for $21.00 ($7.00 each!) and drove it back and forth to Muskegon on weekends for at least a year.

But I was a shy fellow, and during our freshman year I never once set foot in the coffee shop and did little to mix into campus life. For the most part, I went to class and retreated back to our apartment. For our sophomore year the three of us moved to another apartment.

It was during the last two years of college that I came out of my shell. I made many more friends, spent a lot of time mixing in the coffee shop, worked downstairs in the Commons washing dishes, and became a normal college student. I did quite decently in my studies, but certainly didn't stand out at all. The surprise to me at that time is that at the end of my junior year I was elected president of the student council for the next year. For the first time, I think my mind and heart began to sense that it was OK to begin thinking of myself as a leader and my sense of self-confidence slowly began to develop.

Ellie and I were married at the beginning of the summer of 1960 after my first year in seminary and her first year of teaching in the Philadelphia area. Our wedding took place in the Glenside Church in Philadelphia and after a short honeymoon trip in New England, we took up our work in Paterson, New Jersey together. The work in Paterson was good for me, but it did begin the process of convincing me that inner city work was not for me. I saw the crying need for it, recognized the kinds of gifts that would be necessary, but came to realize that my gifts and strengths were not a match for such ministry. For the next two years, I was at seminary and Ellie taught at the Grand Rapids Christian High School. For my second summer assignment we went to the Lebanon Church in Iowa, which providentially became our first pastorate a year later.

Our seminary days brought another level of pain into our lives. It seems a precursor to the fact that significant periods of pain would mark our journey. While other classmates were beginning families, we seemed not able to do so. Some doctoring began and I got a phone call from the doctor one afternoon who bluntly reported that "the chances of you two folks ever having children are pretty darn nil." His bluntness and crassness was offensive and crushing. It was a hint of things to come—that periods of pain and disappointment would mark our journey periodically and that God intended to do his forming work of us through such experiences.

Some months later Ellie was pregnant, but then had a miscarriage before the three-month point. Another disappointment. However, by the time of commencement, she was pregnant again, and nine months later Ron was born—in Sioux Center, Iowa. Eventually, we were blessed with three healthy children.

Graduation from seminary was a time for great celebration. I was glad that school would be done and we were eager for ministry. It turned out that Lebanon extended a call and we were glad to accept it. We moved into the parsonage, and endured my all-day classical examination in First Church in Rock Valley on a Thursday (virtually from 9:00 a.m. till 5:00 p.m.). I passed. The way was cleared for an Ordination Service the next night at Lebanon—September 20, 1962. Our parents were both in town for it, and my uncle, Peter Eldersveld, had come to preach for it. It was a very special time and I was eager to begin my ministry. My first sermons were the next Sunday.

I began with great vigor, only to find that by November I was hospitalized in Sioux Center Hospital with a hemorrhaging ulcer and quite despondent about it all, fearing that maybe I couldn't handle the ministry. It seemed to be one more reminder of the fact that life would involve some significant periods of pain in the midst of blessings and challenges. While recuperating, I got a letter from my Uncle Peter which proved to be prophetic. He had apparently heard from my parents that I was despondent over my hospitalization, and wrote, "Only those who have laid between the two white sheets are ready to do be a good pastor." I received that as very significant advice at the time, but I've thought so often over the years of how true and wise a statement it was—and how formative.

Nearly four years in Lebanon gave me an excellent opportunity to learn how to do ministry and get my feet on the ground with regular preaching.

In 1966 we moved to Trinity Church in Jenison, which I would describe as our happiest and richest pastorate. An older pastor had advised me, in a conversation at synod, that I should be careful where I go for my second pastorate. "The second pastorate," he said, "often sets the tone and character for the rest of our ministry." I tucked it away, and recalled it often. We followed a pastor who had retired but had done little the last few years, so once I came it could go nowhere but up. I was young, energetic, and they thrived on it. It seemed I could not fail. We made many friends and the congregation grew. I feel that I really came into my own as a pastor in Trinity.

But tragedy struck again (as would be the case, it seems, in our lives). Ellie was eight months pregnant with what would be our third child. At a routine appointment, the doctor discovered that the baby had no heartbeat, and she would have to carry it to normal delivery, which turned out to be three weeks later! It was a girl! We were crushed when our daughter was still-born on a Saturday morning. The congregation surrounded us lovingly and supportingly and our bonds deepened. Two fellow pastors assisted in the graveside burial service even while Ellie was still in the hospital. There seemed to be little understanding on the part of the hospital of parent-care in those days. We were really left on our own to manage our grief and we wish now we had had some help from the hospital along the way.

The years at Trinity were six years in which I worked hard and did so almost to the point of burning out. The problem was that I loved the work so much, the congregation was growing well, and I was the only pastor, so I failed to learn how to pace myself and became overworked. This produced some dimensions of depression, and in 1972 I moved to Bethel Church in Lansing, Illinois, and did so partly, I think, to get a new start and disentangle myself from overwork at Trinity Church. My inexperience had not yet allowed me to learn better how to pace myself.

My third pastorate, at Bethel Church, was really a mixture of experiences. On the one hand, I enjoyed being in Chicago and getting acquainted with the big city and feeling its throb. But within five months of arriving there my first diagnosis of cancer took place. It was lymphoma. One more period of pain on the journey! It was devastating for both of us. I had surgery at Rush-Presbyterian-St. Luke's Hospital and then drove in daily for twenty-eight radiation treatments, called cobalt treatments in those days. That whole experience was very disturbing and frightening for us, and also I think for the congregation.

Bethel was my most difficult pastorate. It was a church caught in a dilemma—on the one hand it had developed an excellent neighborhood outreach ministry through women's Bible study groups, the best I have seen in an established church, and many people were deeply committed to it. On the other hand it was a congregation which was suspicious of outreach ministries because they were growing as a congregation. Many of them had moved out of Roseland and Evergreen Park from fear of people of color, so they viewed the growth of Bethel as a threat. When facility expansions were proposed, they looked at it negatively because "it won't be long and we'll all have to move further south again, just like we moved out of Roseland." It was an awful dilemma that created a lot of indecision and pain. This was the setting in which I was able to identify the fact that I do not handle conflict well, and generally try to avoid it. I do not provide helpful ministry in situations that need conflict resolution.

So, in 1978 we moved to Hudsonville to the Hillcrest Church which began a long pastorate of twenty-four years. I never really intended for it to be a long pastorate, but it was just the right thing to do and God kept verifying that fact. Each time I had a call to leave, conversations with the elders indicated I was welcome to continue longer. Those twenty-four years are the heart of my ministry, and much (most!) of who I am is defined by the years at Hillcrest. During those years we developed more staff positions and I learned to grow into a staff ministry; we grew significantly in members; and found the joy of worship with a full sanctuary. The years at Hillcrest were the years of growing worship renewal, with both conflict and satisfaction. Because of that, it became necessary to study and research matters of worship to deal with all the debates and questions that would come up. Two allies were most helpful—a gifted musician on staff as director of music who shared the same vision I had and was an ally in research on it all, and a worship committee which was thoughtful, resourceful and supportive.

During that time several other events took place which significantly formed who I am. Through the addition of other staff ministry positions, I was formed more into a team player, which was a new experience for which I had little preparation. Two more encounters with cancer came—in 1984 and 1990. Again, they were disturbing but also deepening, and they also formed my internal compulsion to make the most of life while I have it. Another period of family pain appeared when Tom, our second son, as an eighth grader developed a swollen neck and was diagnosed with an AVM (arterio-venous malformation) and he urgently needed extensive surgery at Mayo Clinic in Rochester, Minnesota. (This had to be repeated during the early years of his marriage, this time at the University of California, San Diego.) But during this pastorate I also received the privilege of sabbatical leaves of study (three months after every five years of active ministry with a commitment to stay two more years.) This study time gave me the opportunity to earn my ThM from Calvin Seminary, to discover the joy and satisfaction of research and writing, and next to receive my DMin degree from Westminster Seminary in California. These study times provided freshness in ministry and preaching, and increased the trajectory of growth for me personally. It was during this period that I was thrust into the role of public denominational leadership, somewhat unexpectedly to me, at a time of critical denominational conflict over the women-in-office issue. I have been a delegate to Synod, our broadest assembly, ten times in my ministry. In 1988, by surprise, I was elected vice president. The next time I was there, in 1990, I was elected president and completely taken aback by that. Again in 1992 and 1998 I was president, and in 1995 I was first clerk. So for five different synods I was an officer by election. The responsibilities were huge, but it was profoundly reassuring to think of my colleagues saying, "We have a lot of hard work to do, and we want you to lead us through it." I don't think there was anything more thrilling and humbling than an experience like that. I'm sure my record and reputation ever since has been shaped by those events.

But time was moving on and I was getting older. I found that my endurance was shrinking; preaching three times on Sunday was getting to be too much; and having meetings just about every night was increasingly difficult. Yet, I dreaded the idea of retirement and resisted even thinking about it. As I look back, my identity was so completely tied up with being a pastor that I found it too painful to think otherwise. But then the Calvin Institute of Christian Worship was expanding and approached me about the possibility of joining their staff to continue to provide for the larger church the kind of leadership that I had given to Hillcrest and the denomination. Slowly, retirement seemed more attractive and at the end of July 2002, I laid down my role at Hillcrest and the pastorate and began at the Calvin Institute of Christian Worship. As I write this I am still there, representing the Institute at the Seminary.

Sometimes I tire of the question "So when are you going to really retire, Howie?" I do feel that I am retired in many ways. My hours are flexible; I have no evening meetings; I am free on the weekends to be off or to preach somewhere; I don't carry the load of heavy concerns of so many people; and I don't live with the complexity of "running the church." To me, that is retirement, but that doesn't satisfy a lot of folks. I fear they are just too stuck on the American, middle-class expectations of total leisure and pleasure as the ultimate good.

So let me tell you why I am where I am and why I am not eager for a total leisure life. Surely I will have to touch on it later in more extended fashion, but for now allow me to say that I am doing what I desire and love, serving the church, working with ideas, interacting with stimulating people, influencing seminarians, and concentrating on worship. I am in a position where I can for the most part manage my schedule with all its variety. I am in charge of my work and ministry, not the other way around, which is the way it was for forty years. But the largest reason is that I have a philosophy of life that says we have been created by God, redeemed by Christ, gifted by the Holy Spirit, to be of service, and this calling remains lifelong. And besides, I don't think God would have healed me from cancer three times just to give me years of leisure—he did it so I could serve and to show my thanks to him by doing so. Frankly, when my first encounter with cancer occurred in 1972, I assumed I would not live long and certainly would never reach retirement. Well, here I am, nearly fifteen years past retirement, more than forty years past that first cancer encounter, and very healthy. I give my thanks to God by serving him in these ways. I know the time will come when it will be necessary for me to lay all this down, either because my health (or lack of it) no longer allows for this, or because there is no longer a place for me here, but until then I will serve as I am able. And when people ask, "When are you going to retire?" I'll just smile!

Well, it's been quite a journey. I hope you can see that woven into my life story are significant events and experiences that were essentially formational in tone. Many of them seemed only painful at the time; not until later did I begin to recognize the hand of God that was shaping and refining this common ordinary man from Muskegon for significant service in the kingdom. I write this to you because I hope the same is true on your journey and that you will increasingly recognize the shaping hand of God in our experiences.

In my further letters I'd like to take you back into some of my experiences and reflections so you can walk with me through God's grooming process . . . and perhaps see more clearly what he may be doing in you to make you a better servant of his.

In Christian Service,
Your Colleague

Thinking About It—

> What are some of the key turning points in your journey that have formed you?

> In what surprising ways has God formed you?

2

An Expanding Call

Dear Pastor,

At Calvin Seminary, we have the practice of frequently asking students to tell us their "calling story"—are you called, how did your sense of calling develop, and what type or direction of calling is it? I think we all know that's a pretty foundational matter and greatly shapes our motivation for ministry, and there are times when the demands and the stress of the Christian ministry are so great, it is only our sense of calling that will hold us there.

My sense of calling arose in a rather unique way that I ought to explain. On the one hand it was very simple, but compared with many it was quite unique. It developed in several stages and so I think of it as a growing call. Actually there were about four stages in the process. First there was my basic calling to the ministry which took place very early, and God convicted me that my life was to be used lifelong in the gospel ministry. Other vocations were to be out of view and I was to be in the Christian ministry. As I matured I came to realize that such a commitment involved placing my entire life at the service of the gospel and the church. However, clarification of that calling was still needed. What all would this involve? The first step of clarification put emphasis on the work of preaching. The process of calling continued and I came to see that the calling to be a pastor was also to be an integral part of my ministry. A pastor has a loving and committed bond with the people of the church. The minister cares for them and preaches to them because he/she is their pastor. And then midway through my ministry I gradually came to identify that, in addition to preaching and pastoring, the planning and leading of worship was also essential. Worship is to be central in the life of the church, and therefore central in the life and work of the minister. So, the process began by receiving a call from God to ministry, followed by a continued refinement or shaping my personal identity in such a way that I couldn't help but recognize it as multidimensional, involving each of these other roles. In the pages ahead I will explore what those four dimensions involve—ministry, preaching, pastoring and worshiping. Ministry is the broadest term, an overarching concept of being in service to the gospel and the church. The other three more specifically identify the areas involved in the work of ministry, like the three legs on which a stool stands.

When we ask seminarians about their story, we learn that every story is different. Some of them speak excitedly about it with such clarity. Others seem reticent to address the matter because it's still shrouded in a degree of uncertainty. Most of them seem to find their calling gradually clarified through a variety of life experiences, and some of them enter seminary as a second career, some even in midlife.

My story is unique, as is each story of calling. Perhaps you will be able to reassess your sense of calling by listening to mine. Maybe it's all very clear to you. Or maybe you are one of those who continues to wrestle with some of these issues.

I can truthfully say that I was determined, in my own heart, to be a minister from nearly the fourth grade on. I'm confident I felt that way because God planted it there. Maybe it was even earlier, but I don't have much memory of that. In those days being a "minister" and being a "preacher" were synonymous. So I would go up to my room to "write a sermon" at my desk. If anyone asked, I always said, "I want to be a preacher." Nothing else seemed to enter my mind—oh, except those childhood fantasies of wanting to be a fireman or a jet pilot! So I never really wavered in that, and everyone who knew me knew that I wanted to be a preacher. It was a forgone conclusion I would be going on from high school to Calvin College, and then to Calvin Theological Seminary. Nothing else was even considered. It was a straight track for me, from high school right through seminary.

As I look back I can identify three influences that probably led to that, though I acknowledge that God's sovereign leading was surely behind it all. My grandfather was a minister, and though I don't remember much of him because he died when I was only a few years old, I think the spirit in our family of "grandpa the preacher" held up a noble model for me. The second tangible influence was Uncle Pete (Eldersveld) who was not only a preacher, but the radio minister of the Back to God Hour. He was a revered leader of the church; a fine model for a young fellow like me; and he would give me much encouragement along the way. But he was also free to challenge me, saying at times, "Well, if you are going to be a preacher, then be a good one; we've already got too many of the other kind!" But I think the third influence, much more intangible, was that my parents were church members who were regularly friends with our pastor. My father was frequently an elder, and even when not in office as an elder he was very active in church, so his relationship with our current pastor was always a good one, and the pastor was a frequent guest in our home. As I grew up, therefore, I was able to get to know our pastors on a personal basis. They were personal, respected family friends. I'm sure that influenced my own desire to be one.

So I started Calvin College, naturally, as a pre-seminary student. Studies went well and I felt very confirmed in it. The result of being a pre-sem student is that my identity was immediately shaped by that. I associated with other pre-sems, made pre-sem friends, and in general the die was cast. However, when I got into my sophomore year the questions I had never faced began to surface—"I will have no other major, so I will be unmarketable in any other field if I change my mind. I better be sure now, before I go any farther." I wrestled with it for most of a semester, and even considered changing to a sociology major, even criminal justice (telling myself that maybe I'd want to be a prison warden!). I wrote a letter to one of my former pastors spelling out my quandary. His advice was that since I had sensed this call since being a child I better keep going unless I had a very good reason for changing. "Gehen sie an," he wrote in German. So I kept going. And the struggle seemed to vanish from that point on. It was good advice.

So I came to see that as the first step of my calling. It was only the beginning; yet to come was a sense of identity that would express what kind of calling I had received. My first pastorate was a rural congregation in northwest Iowa, Lebanon Church. I was pleased at that. It was the kind of place I wanted for my first venture into the ministry.

But there were still many other questions to be answered about the type of calling I had received. Was it to be pastor of an established congregation, a home missionary, world missionary, or a chaplain? Whereas seminarians have so many more options open to them today, those four were about the only possibilities that I could consider. I had received a number of pastoral calls while in Lebanon to different types of ministries and with each the struggle came all over again—what kind of a calling do I have?

Gradually, the other dimension of my calling became clear. It was much slower to come than my initial call. Early on I just assumed I was "going into the ministry to be a preacher." But gradually the concept of *pastor* squeezed its way into the picture. The word *pastor* answered the question of why I would want to be a minister, and what I'd like to do in that role. The answer was "to pastor God's people." It also gave me a metaphor around which I could arrange my entire ministry. The one core idea that characterized it all and held it all together was the idea of caring for them. The word *pastor* always has been a very warm and rich word for me. It spoke not only of a task but also of a relationship. To pastor someone means to shepherd them and Psalm 23 seemed to be the best model. As a shepherd, the Lord cares for us, renews us, protects us, feeds us with resources, and gives us eternal treasures. So to pastor someone means to have compassion for them and that picture comes from Matthew 9:36, for Jesus "had compassion on them, because they were harassed and helpless like sheep without a shepherd." A pastor, therefore, is a deep-feeling and deeply committed person. To pastor people means not only to care for them, but to rescue them from danger and distress. In Luke 15:1–7, the good shepherd seeks for the lost sheep until he finds it and then rejoices while he brings it home. To pastor means to feed the sheep of the congregation. In John 21, when Jesus gives Peter his commission it is to "feed my sheep." But underneath it all, I believe that to pastor means to have a deep caring relationship with someone. In John 10, Jesus explains that the Shepherd knows his sheep by name, calls them, and leads them. They, in turn, know his voice and follow him. I looked at the members of the congregation whom I was called to serve and increasingly I would refer to them as "my people." They belonged to me. I belonged to them. It was a "pastoral relationship." And so I knew that my job description meant doing for them whatever good pastoring would involve. I would love them, support them in trying experiences, visit them, enjoy them, pray for them, and even confront them . . .

I'm sure that the modeling I had seen influenced this concept a great deal. I came to realize that, in spite of the fact that my home church was not a particularly healthy church, I did recognize that those who served us had been excellent pastors. So I had good modeling, but I also came to realize that this role fit my personality best. I was a person who cared, who had deep feelings, and who had been shaped by my family to care for those who were needy.

At the time, of course, I didn't realize the full cost involved in being a pastor to someone. It involved becoming incarnate for them, meeting them where they were, knowing their names, taking on their concerns, listening to them, praying for them, feeling their pain, sharing their joys, standing by their bedside, at their graveside, marrying them, baptizing them, breaking bread and pouring juice for them, and hearing their concerns about family and children.

Over the years of serving in the pastorate, I learned that it involved some large privileges and gave me the opportunity to have a front row seat to so many of the big things God was doing in their lives. When you are a pastor you hear things like these:

- Pastor, my mother just died.
- We're going to have a baby.
- The doctor told me the CT scan doesn't look good at all.
- We'll be moving this summer.
- Our family prays for you regularly.
- Thanks for being there when we needed you.
- My husband just left me.
- I'd like to profess my faith.
- Thanks for the sermon.
- Pastor, I just can't seem to pray anymore.
- My son refuses to go to church anymore.
- Pastor, will you marry us?
- I just can't get past the nagging feeling that God has let me down.

The list is endless, but it's a front row seat to life among God's people.

And as that concept became more and more clear, something else became clear. You can't be a preacher unless you are a pastor (a distant preacher is an oxymoron) and the most effective pastoral ministry also involves preaching.

So my sense of calling involved both dimensions—to preach and to pastor. They developed at different rates at different times and in different manners. But the two have and need a collegial relationship in the whole process, through seminary, and all through the ministry of my four pastorates. The responsibilities have gotten heavy at times; I've become discouraged and frustrated at other times; but I have never seriously doubted my sense of calling. So here I am in the final chapter of life, still in the ministry, still preaching, still being a pastor.

But when I tell seminarians about my sense of calling they seem somewhat surprised. Some are surprised that it was that clear and that early. They can't imagine knowing it as a child. Others are surprised at how long it took for the full concept to come to clarity. First was the calling to ministry, but it was a process of years until ministry took the shape of "pastor" and then "preacher" and finally "worship leader."

I wonder about you and what your experiences have been. I wonder if your sense of calling is sure in your own heart, or if there are times when you still feel quite uncertain about it. And I wonder how clarified the different roles are in your heart.

I cannot stress strongly enough how strategically important a firm sense of calling is. How could I stand before a congregation and dare to speak for God if I have no sense of calling to do so? How could I step into the personal experiences of people's lives at all different points if I am not convinced that God wants me there? How could I ever hope to bear the burden of ministry in tough times if I am not convinced I am where God wants me to be? How could I resist the temptation to walk away from heavy and painful circumstances unless deep within me is the conviction that I am where God wants me to be?

In His Service,
Your Colleague

Thinking About It—

What is your view of "pastoring"?

What has God done to shape your pastor-heart?

3

Privileged to Preach

Dear Pastor,

In my previous letter, I said that *ministry* and *preaching* and *pastoring* go together, though it took a process of years for me to identify all that. A life given in commitment to the gospel and the church is a life that is given to the preaching of the Word and its gospel, and caring for God's people.

Preaching and sermons, therefore, have always been a huge part of my life. I remember that, as a young child, I would fantasize about "being a preacher." Now I have a file of them in my basement that pack eight drawers in my filing cabinets. For some sentimental reason I just can't seem to get rid of them. And by this time in my life I have preached just slightly more than four thousand times. And then add funerals, and other settings of delivering a "devotional/meditation" and it's clear that I've been called to preach. People would come from all walks of life and all kinds of experiences during the week and they would expect to hear something fresh, wise, helpful, and engaging week after week. Expectations like that are enough to stir panic in the soul of a preacher.

I wonder what your feelings are on that matter. Are you in love with the hard task of preaching? Perhaps my thoughts will help you assess your convictions and feelings about it.

I have loved preaching and considered it to be the heart of my work in ministry. All else could be subject to "benign neglect," but never preaching. I loved it, always sought to do it well, worked hard at it, found that preaching well was tantalizing, sometimes mystifying, always draining, and yet very satisfying. So I worked hard at it, regularly read books about how to preach, and often attended conferences and workshops on preaching. But I never felt I fully conquered the task or fully understood it. I would like to believe that I have been recognized as a pretty good preacher and that my four congregations assessed me that way, but I realize now that I've only made a start of it. Here at the seminary now I realize that, though I worked hard at it, with some gifts for it, my preaching has the marks of a previous generation.

Preaching is a demanding task. I'm appalled at some today who seem to get away with a short sermon (allegedly because people have a short attention span) and who seem OK with giving their sermon a short supply of hard work. I'm even surprised at the seminarians and preachers who talk, with a sense of self-pity, about what a heavy load it is to bring a sermon week-after-week, when I and my generation had to bring two every week (and on occasion, three!). For the final fifteen years of my ministry I wrote two sermons and preached three times a Sunday most weeks—the morning sermon at 8:30 service and 11:00 service, and the evening sermon at 5:30 p.m. I discovered very early in my ministry that a good sermon on Sunday required self-disciplined study time during the week. Since I am a morning person, and do my best studying in the morning hours, I made the commitment early that my mornings would be "sermon time" and interruptions were to be only when absolutely necessary. No appointments, no calls, no other meetings during the morning hours. I would even announce this to the congregation so they would be considerate and not interrupt, and they could also be assured that their pastor was preparing well for his sermons.

I am not an academician and homiletical theory is not my strong suit. I have learned how to study and exegete a text, how to structure a message well, and how to write a message so that it is persuasive and interesting. But when it comes to analyzing and critiquing different homiletical methods, I'll take a pass and adapt my method in a way that fits the passage, suits the audience, carries out the intent of the text, and is consistent with who I am and what my gifts are. Yet, I was consistently amazed and enriched to become increasingly aware of the variety found on the pages of Scripture—in its type of literature, the genre of text, historical context, intent and purpose, and the personalities of the human authors. The faithful student of Scripture will find no limit to the resources for rich preaching material.

My homiletical training at Calvin Seminary was good. It was solid, but not exciting. The excitement was to be found in my pastorate, as week by week I explored the work for this great privilege of preaching. Both my education and the rigors of preaching weekly did stir in me the desire to keep on learning lifelong. So I read what other preachers wrote about the task. I developed a large desire for reading sermons. I joined a tape club and received a cassette every month of two sermons and eagerly devoured them. I then decided that my graduate work would be in homiletics. I received the ThM degree from Calvin Seminary on the basis of a thesis that examined the radio sermons of Peter Eldersveld on the Back to God Hour—*A Voice for the Historic Christian Faith*. After that I pursued my DMin degree at Westminster Seminary and focused on advanced planning in preaching by studying the needs of the congregation in addition to studying the text, and then put my ideas together in a book, *Preaching That Connects*. I don't consider it to be a major work, or even an excellent book, but it was a key part of my growth.

All along the way I kept analyzing my own preaching. I learned from some writers that sermons ought to be a balanced diet of one-third each from the Old Testament, the Gospels, and the Epistles. But when I studied the record of my own preaching I discovered I was out of balance, with little Old Testament and too much Epistles. So alterations were needed. About halfway through my ministry I learned the discipline and benefit of writing a complete manuscript and found that method enabled me to hone the craft even more, though the challenge for me was to write a complete manuscript yet not take it into the pulpit with me. Some preachers seem able to preach from a full manuscript without distraction and I admire them for it. I, however, could not. I always feared that eyes on a manuscript would interfere with my rapport with listeners. I experimented with a variety of styles of preaching—more biographical, narrative, problem-oriented, and confessional. I even did some first-person sermons. Along the way I became very convinced of the value of series of sermons on a common theme and much of my preaching reflected this approach. The congregation regularly expected series of four to twelve sermons each.

I found great satisfaction in planning ahead in my preaching schedule. I had "hoppers," files on my desk, with an assortment of ideas and notes for sermons and series in the future. I found it particularly satisfying to go to the library at a couple of neighboring colleges where I could study uninterrupted for an afternoon or two each week, hiding away with all my sermon material to plot out a season or a series of sermons. Consequently I always had a dozen or two sermons in various stages of development.

And I also came to value the insight and suggestions that the elders of the church contributed toward my preaching. In our monthly meetings, we frequently discussed my preaching and how well it was meeting the needs of the congregation. I took them into the discussions about planning for sermons and sermon series. Twice a year I'd present them with a list of suggestions for sermons and ask them to evaluate them in terms of what should be included. I developed a "Situational Analysis Form" which they received annually with a long list of themes/topics to be addressed in preaching and I asked them to select those which were most needed in the life of this congregation at present. The feedback I received was consistently valuable.

So it's been a lifelong journey of loving to preach, studying how to preach better, and eagerly looking forward to Sunday as the peak of the week. I could approach Scripture and know I was finding truth that would never let me down. I could write a sermon on it and know it was built on truth that would last. I also never wavered in my belief that the Holy Spirit aimed to use preaching to do his work, even sermons that were less than they should be, and I believed that when good did come from those sermons, it was because the Holy Spirit was using them to nurture faith. My task was to prepare the Word in a listenable form, set it out there, and allow the Holy Spirit to use it. Yet in all my searching for how to do it better, one thing never changed. I never wavered in my firm conviction that the Bible is the inspired Word of God and I served God's people best when I faithfully brought them his Word each week. I could find no greater privilege, and yet it would always challenge me, tantalize me, and drive me on.

Yes, in all my preaching work, I remain fascinated at the anomaly of it all. Here is a task that seems so important, is declared to be so powerful, can be so satisfying, and yet at the same time seems so unconquerable. I have preached for over fifty years now and still have not come to fully understand it. I preach what I think is a pretty good sermon and it receives a somewhat mediocre response. The next week I preach one that seems fair-at-best, and great appreciation comes through. And in it all I never tire of thinking about Paul's word in 1 Corinthians 1:18, "The message of the cross is foolishness to those who are perishing, but to us who are being saved, it is the power of God." I read that verse, and remember that God has called me to preach, and I get tears in my eyes and a lump in my throat. I wonder how and why God has chosen and called me for such a profound task, and I feel humbled and awed at the unique privilege I have been given.

Being a preacher has been a high and holy privilege. Standing before the people of God and saying, "Here is the Word of God," is a privilege that is second to none. We may be weary and exhausted on Sunday night and Monday morning, but there is no better way to spend one's life.

I hope your sense of calling to ministry is sure, but I also hope you are filled with a sense of awe at the privilege of preaching God's Word. And I also hope you never come to the point where you feel you have mastered it. Instead, keep growing, keep trusting, and keep relying on God to do his work through your efforts.

In His Service,
Your Colleague

Thinking About It—

What is the most challenging part of preaching for you?

What is the most satisfying part of preaching for you?

4

Worship at the Center

DEAR PASTOR,

About halfway through my ministry, the church experienced an earthquake in its worship life. Worship renewal became the theme of the day, fueled at least partly by the Second Vatican Council. Churches began looking at their worship with critical eyes, asking questions they had never thought to ask before, desiring a freshness and creativity from worship leaders. I sensed very soon that the shape of my ministry and its responsibilities was undergoing profound change. Today it doesn't take long before a pastor comes to realize that worship is a big concern in ministry. If you are a pastor, you likely are involved in planning and leading the weekly worship services. And I trust you realize that vibrant worship is the key to much of the spiritual health of the congregation. But you've probably also come to recognize that worship is the source of occasional conflict and tension. Perhaps you've been involved in some of the discussions and debates which reflect different viewpoints and preferences about worship matters. So sorting through some of our thoughts about our worship ministry seems very necessary.

It's obvious to just about everyone today that worship and worship styles are the subject of great diversity and differences of opinion. Surely you've run into that in your ministry. It seems that no leader can escape it today.

For generations, worship services generally followed the same pattern week after week. Little variation was involved, creativity was unheard of, and questions about the liturgy, its structure, flexibility, and music were rarely discussed. Worship committees, if they existed, were placid places. But soon the landscape shifted and the mood in the churches became quite different. Churches began to feel the sweep of a desire for diversity, the shift toward the contemporary, and soon worship changes were the mood of the day. Some churches began to identify themselves by their worship style. Others became a nest of indecision and tension. And pastors were often caught in the middle. We learned, and began to use, some new words—"worship wars" and "worship renewal." In the midst of such a situation, the pastor is called to give leadership. It is no easy task.

It was in the midst of these profound changes in the life of the church that I came to realize that "ministry" involved not only preaching and pastoring, but also worshiping. My concept of the role of minister broadened out to see that worship leading and worship planning were to be at the center of ministry in the same way that worship was to be at the center of the life of the church. Worship, after all, is God's plan for his church. He calls us to worship. There is no hour of the week that is quite as strategic for the body of Christ as that hour when it gathers in the presence of God for worship. And there is no hour that is as strategic for the minister as that hour when such a large part of the family gathers for worship.

This work of planning and leading worship would, of course, be much simpler if the Bible had given us a clear and concise set of specific worship practices that we are to follow. Instead, we are provided with a handful of principles that we are left to implement in our local setting.

Though the viewpoints on just what these principles are and what they mean will vary from one congregation and pastor to another, major and trusted students of the Bible point to principles such as these:

- Worship generally takes the form of a dialog or conversation with God which takes place at God's initiative. God invites us; he has the first word; and our role is that of respondent. He is the initiator of grace; we are the recipients.

- The vertical relationship, between God and worshipers, is more important than the horizontal relationship between worshipers.

- Vibrant worship will involve full and active participation by all participants. God acts through his Word, call, blessing and grace. Worshipers act through their praise, prayers, responses, and commitments.

- True worship is Trinitarian in nature even as God is Triune. The Father who calls us, the Son who redeems us, and the Spirit who empowers us each participate in worship for the benefit of those who are his children.

- True worship is centered around the Word and the Sacraments. God has come to reveal himself to us in his Word, and he extends his grace to us through the sacraments of Holy Baptism and the Lord's Supper.

- Music in worship intends to be the expression of the believer's heart and soul. In music the spirit of the believer speaks and responds to God and his Word, reflecting on life and its experiences, and seeking grace and care.

- Worship is to be inclusive of all those who come. Age, gender, gifts, abilities, and all other considerations are not to be hindrances but rather to be eagerly welcomed and included.

- Those who worship God do so with a fervent desire and passion that others will come to join them also. They do not consider their worship closed, but rather desire that others will recognize the presence of God here and come to join the conversation.

- Worship is to give expression to the full range of human experience. The Psalms are our pattern, where joy and delight, praise and thanks, confession and intercession, lament and sorrow all find their expressions coming from the worshipers.

There are other principles also that you may desire to add. Many of them will be suggested and shaped by the culture of which you are a part and by the personality and history of your congregation.

As a pastor, you will be called to provide leadership to your worshiping congregation and this will prove to be a rich privilege but also a complex and at times frustrating task. You will value the participation and support of other knowledgeable leaders either on staff or in lay leadership positions. You will be grateful for a congregation that will reflect, think, study and grow in its understanding of worship. You will be served well by your own care in studying, researching and participating in conferences that will upgrade your understanding of Christian worship. The ability to listen will become increasingly important as you attempt to help people with conflicting opinions understand each other.

Though leading a congregation when there are tensions over worship questions is a difficult task, we must never lose sight of three fundamental convictions. First, God desires his people to worship him. Worship is his idea and he is honored and glorified when his people worship him well. Worship, therefore, is not optional, but is part of our obedience to God. And our ministries of worship leadership, therefore, are an act on our part of giving to God the honor he deserves by drawing his people together before him in vibrant worship. And, second, the responsibility of planning and leading worship for a congregation of believers is a high and holy privilege. When we worship we are on sacred ground. As prophets we bring the word of the Lord to them; as priests we stand between them and God to bring their needs and cares to God. When the task brings weariness we are apt to lose sight of this but reminders are regularly needed. And, third, the fact that worship involves so many issues, questions, and opinions today brings a large challenge to pastors. Faithfully meeting that challenge will happen best if we always bear several considerations in mind. Because of the sacredness of worship we serve our congregation best when we enable them to worship thoughtfully and actively. Because questions and confusion are so prevalent in our congregations today, our educational task is great. We should be able to teach and inform them of the principles of biblical worship as stated above. Because of the intensity of worship debates and the firmness with which many hold to their opinions on worship, we should model the practices of listening well and collaborating patiently, while holding to foundational principles. Hopefully we can therefore help a congregation rise above conflict, reach understanding with each other, and continue to treasure the right to come into the presence of God.

Along with each of these reminders, the worship leader must be careful to protect the personal practice of worshiping while leading. It is far too easy to be preoccupied with the activity of worship than to engage in the essence of worship. Our calling requires us to plan and lead worship well, while our hearts need us to engage well in worship while we lead.

In His Service,
Your Colleague

Thinking About It—

> What are the "hot button" issues in your congregation that threaten the vibrancy of your worship life?
>
> Review the principles cited above. Which are observed well in your congregation? Which need some reinforcement and how can you best do that?

5

Learning to Work

Dear Pastor,

At times there is an elephant in the room of a pastorate—a big issue that few people will address openly. It's the work ethic, the ability to work hard, and the degree of self-discipline that the pastor/preacher needs. To be sure, we hear some off-handed comments from time to time by some parishioners about only working hard one day a week and the rest of it being quite easy. But that's certainly not true, at least for pastor/preachers who are faithful and have successful ministries. The ability to work hard while unsupervised is key. No one is there to watch us, to note what hours we keep, how many hours we put in each week, or to keep track of how much time we take off. Frankly, it's easy to be undisciplined in the ministry because time is our own.

As I look back, I'm grateful that I've always had a positive attitude toward hard work. I enjoy working. I enjoy the productivity that results from it. I detest being unprepared for certain tasks, or feeling like I haven't done my best. I'm more conscious of that now that I'm in this chapter called retirement and still find joy in being productive. I've been working at the seminary here for a number of years and increasingly I realize that I find joy in working and being productive. Sometimes when friends ask if I'm still working here, my answer to them is a surprise. When I tell them I am here five days a week, they react with "really?" And then I feel the need to justify it. Yet, I enjoy doing so; I am happiest when I can get up in the morning and have a regular schedule of work waiting for me; when I can commute to the seminary, open up my office, and look ahead to the day knowing that I'll be engaged in meaningful activities and relationships. It's very satisfying to me. Though, to be sure, primarily because of my age, my days are much shorter now than they have been before, and include much less stress.

I'm sure my ability to work is stirred by several considerations:

- My health, because I think I am healthier than most of my peers and by remaining active I'm expressing my gratitude for good health.

- My position, for being a part of the Institute of Worship and Calvin Seminary is certainly a noble task and an opportunity to make a difference.

- My contacts and relationships, at the staff at the Calvin Institute of Christian Worship and Calvin Theological Seminary are a great group to be part of and I've developed many good friendships here.

- My influence, for here I have the opportunity to teach, mentor and interact with students in a way that will shape their ministries for the sake of the church of Christ.

- I suppose one other consideration is my personal work ethic: I simply don't believe that people are designed to sit around unproductively, and a retirement of such inactivity would drive me nuts. So it's also my philosophy of life that keeps me working.

And from time to time I find myself wondering, "How was it that I learned to work?" I find it valuable to identify the experiences I've had along the way, all of which shaped me. I encourage you to do that, too. I'm sure my father and our family culture had a lot to do with that. The Vanderwells were an impoverished immigrant family with ten children. When they arrived here from Europe they all had to work hard in the factories in Muskegon to help make ends meet. My father, therefore, was a hard worker from his early teen years when he first went to the factory, through his entire career at Sealed Power Piston Rings. I rarely heard him complain about it, though I know there were times when he was very frustrated and wished he could have gotten into something else (he spoke about his dream to be a school teacher). But he faithfully worked hard and was recognized for that. It was obvious that he took delight in good work done well. I relish recalling the time when he took each of us boys to work with him for a full day in our senior year of high school. He gave us a tour of the Sealed Power factory, beginning in the foundry first thing in the morning, all the way through the process of making and shaping piston rings, so that we ended up at the shipping dock at 3:00 p.m. Then he'd take us home, put milk and a cookie in front of us, and drive home his point, "Now you see what life in a factory is like; so when you have an opportunity for your education, be sure you make the most of it, do your best to find a challenging vocation." I've never forgotten that lesson.

But I was also shaped by the various jobs I had already in my teen years. My first work was a summer job on the celery fields for a friend of my parents. We cut and crated celery in the muck fields from Whitehall to Muskegon. We'd start early in the morning, work all day, get thirsty and hungry, and find it very boring. But when my first paycheck came at $22.00 I was delighted. My next job in the mid-teens was for a small neighborhood grocery store in Muskegon. I stocked shelves, carried out groceries, arranged overstock in the basement, delivered handbills to the neighborhood, and then on Friday and Saturday I would take his car and deliver the orders of groceries that people had called in. Since I was barely sixteen years old, I really liked driving his car, an Oldsmobile. In high school, I moved up to a larger supermarket. I worked there all through high school and I must have been a good and faithful worker because I kept moving up from one job to another. First I stocked shelves and carried out groceries, then I helped the produce department, and finally was promoted to work in the meat department. There I could wait on customers at the counter, cut beef, grind hamburger, and eventually was able to "break down" a quarter of beef, either the front quarter or hind quarter so it would be ready for sale in the counter or for custom orders. I really enjoyed working in that place, put in as many hours as I could while I was in school, and particularly enjoyed being in the meat department. To this day, I like being able to cut up some beef, pork, or a chicken.

Once I went to college, I needed a job on campus and so I began to work in the kitchen (scullery) washing dishes—taking dishes and trays as the students brought them in, sorting them out, and running them through the dishwasher. It was messy, smelly, had very little dignity, but I made friends there and felt like I was doing my part. During the summers of college, I had what proved to be my most challenging and interesting job. My brother Russ worked for Sanitary Dairy delivering milk on a house-to-house route. They needed vacation drivers to relieve drivers for a week or two for vacation time. So each summer I would take four different routes, spend one week with the driver to "learn it" and then take it ten days or two weeks on my own, and then move on to the next route. I enjoyed driving the stand-up Divco milk trucks; I even didn't mind getting up about 4:00 a.m. and starting early; and I liked the idea of getting to know so many people and so many different parts of the city. I worked hard at that job, a lot of lifting, and never could quite establish the pace and speed with which a regular driver could cover his route. So at times I was quite behind schedule. I received good encouragement and I could save nearly enough to be ready for college in the fall. The problem was that the early morning schedule went with me to college, and I was wide awake by 4:00 in the morning, and by 3:00 in the afternoon was very ready for a nap. It took a month or two to make that transition.

So vigorous work, physical and mental, has always been a part of my life. While serving in Lebanon, Iowa, I delighted to have Mondays in which I could go to the farm of a parishioner and work with him in the field, on the tractor, or in the yard. Even the physical work in the yard that I enjoy now is an expression of that. I'm not afraid of it, and I heartily enjoy being productive. That's partly my philosophy of life, partly my upbringing, partly my experiences of employment . . . and perhaps some other things too of which I'm not even aware.

So I'm grateful that I have learned the joy of working and being productive. I'm grateful for good health that makes it possible. And I realize that the willingness to work is key to any kind of success in life . . . and ministry. I write about this for your awareness. I've seen colleagues of mine whose work habits have been very healthy, and those who are otherwise. Some with poor self-discipline pay the price for it and their ministry suffers. Others who have learned the joy of productivity not only find satisfaction in their ministry but tend to have ministries that are more productive.

In His Service,
Your Colleague

Thinking About It—

> What work ethic issues do you face?
>
> How would you characterize your work ethic?
>
> How do you think leaders of your congregation would characterize it? Does that matter?

6

Our Attitude of Heart

Dear Pastor,

There is another problem that all pastors face. It's one they likely will not tell you about. As a matter of fact, they hardly even admit this one to themselves. It's the one about their attitude, or rather let's say it's about the size of their ego. You know what egotism is, don't you? It's the practice of thinking too much of our self, of referring to our self too often. We all have an ego, but those who are afflicted with egotism have a rather inflated ego. They think too much of themselves.

This is a dangerous struggle. There are certain professions which seem uniquely groomed to increase the size of our ego. As you think about that I'm sure that you can easily identify a number of them. Well, the Christian ministry would be among them.

We might think it wouldn't be that way. After all, as ministers/pastors we are to be Christlike, and it is beyond dispute that if anyone embodied humility more than anything else it would be Christ. Christ emptied himself and he gave himself in service that was selfless. And that is to be our model.

But, as you well know, this is not a perfect world and things easily get distorted. The pastor is subject to such distortion, just like others. Like the disciples, we forget that he emptied himself, that he came to serve, not to be served. But, instead they were more concerned about who would be the greatest in the kingdom of heaven.

Just think how repeatedly we are tempted to fall into that ego trap. When we speak, people tend to listen a little more carefully because the pastor is speaking. We have a title and everyone knows that. In town they call us "Reverend." At a meeting we are the one they turn to for the opening prayer. When we deliver a sermon, hundreds come to listen, and at the close of it we normally go to the door to receive their comments about how wonderful the message was.

And in all of this, what happens to our ego? Does it not become just a little more inflated each time? Doesn't our self-concept, our idea of who we are, of the treatment we ought to receive, of how we ought to be listened to, or the credit we deserve, or the respect we can command, step up a notch . . . or three? In short, we think of ourselves more highly than we ought to think.

And therein lies the problem for us. You would think not, but it happens so gradually that we hardly even notice it. First, we receive the respect and comments from folks gratefully. Then we come to expect them more and more. We depend on them. And finally it reshapes our concept of who we are, of the treatment we ought to expect, of how folks ought to listen to us, of the credit we deserve, and the respect we can commandeer. In short we think more highly of ourselves than we ought to think. And before long our self-concept, our idea of who we are, has become elevated. Our ego has become inflated. We have placed our self on a pedestal. We have fallen victim to egotism, and we have left humility behind.

And in the process we make the mistake of forgetting what the Bible has taught us, and what we have taught others, about humility. We have forgotten the teaching of Proverbs that "humility comes before honor" (15:33); and we have forgotten that the prophet Micah has said that the Lord requires of us "to walk humbly with your God" (6:8); and we've also forgotten the words of Paul, to "clothe yourselves with . . . humility" (Col 3:12), and of Peter, who exhorts church leaders to "humble yourselves, therefore, under God's mighty hand, that he may lift you up in due time" (1 Pet 5:5). And it means we've probably lost sight of David's exclamation when the Lord renewed his promise to him that he would make his name great, for instead of pride there was the exclamation, "Who am I, O Lord, and what is my family, that you have brought me this far?" (2 Sam 7:18). These are great models for us as we shape our attitude of mind. And so is Paul when he reminds us, "Do not think of yourself more highly than you ought" (Rom 12:3), and John the Baptist, who pledged, "He must become greater; I must become less" (John 3:30).

Can you sense the quiet, subtle, but terribly profound shift in attitude that often takes place? The servant of Christ is called to be Christlike in all humility. But often that doesn't happen. Instead, those who ought to be pointing to Christ are pointing to themselves; and those who are pledged to make him increase, instead are quite pleased when they increase. And the very people who ought to be saying, "I am only a servant of Christ, trying to do my best," instead are saying, "I am important; look to me and listen to me!"

It is with good reason that I give you strong warning against this error, for it is dangerous indeed. If we are to be Christlike as we represent him, this attitude of heart that is twisted into a focus on our own ego, serves to mutilate any Christlikeness that may reside in us.

Not only does it destroy Christlikeness. It also destroys our influence as a pastor/leader. People in the church generally have a harder time listening to leaders who are so full of themselves that they normally find it more attractive to talk about themselves than about Christ. And so similarly, most church members, to say nothing of seekers or inquirers, will find it even harder to listen. And along with such tragedies, we must note that a swollen ego makes worship much more difficult. It's more difficult for those of us who are the leaders, because when we are so full of ourselves we hardly have room for Christ to be in first place and it's also hard for good worship to happen under those circumstances. In addition there is the major problem of getting followers to eagerly join us in worship when we are so full of ourselves. It sabotages worship at its heart.

Perhaps we can make that last statement a key statement with which to conclude this chapter. Pastors/leaders who are so filled with themselves that they have left humility far behind will find their me-first attitude of heart will eventually sabotage most of what is very good in their ministry.

In His Service,
Your Colleague

Thinking About It—

> Identify two previous leaders who have had a major influence on you—one who had a positive influence because he/she was Christlike with humility. And the other who had a negative influence because you sense he/she was too enthused about themselves.

> Select one or two very trusted friends with whom you can be fully accountable. Ask them to share honest reflections about yourself. Then solicit their responses to these two questions: where in my behavior and leadership do I portray Christlike humility?

> And where do you see an attitude of mind that portrays pride, and too much emphasis on my own ego? (Remember that such conversations can easily be destroyed by defensiveness on your part. The only two responses to their comments on your part should be "tell me more" and "thank you.")

7

Surviving as an Introvert

DEAR PASTOR,

While we are talking about the concepts and the calling that formed me for ministry, I should also address the matter of my personality because I know it's something you'll have to face too. God forms us for ministry, I am convinced, also by taking into consideration the type of personality we have. I have had to make peace with who I am. I also needed to accept the fact that who I am will shape my ministry and how I serve. That becomes a bit difficult when we don't really know who we are, and when we discover it, don't really like it.

Over the years I had taken many personality tests and temperament analyses. They all came highly recommended and I found a certain amount of value in each of them, but I never reached the point of realizing "There! That's who I am and that's what I'm like!" My identity makeup always remained shrouded in a bit of mystery and uncertainty. I came to realize that I didn't fit in any neat, simple category. I knew early on, by comparing myself with others near to me, that I was never going to be the outgoing type who would delight in striking up a conversation with others. Ellie and I could visit with parishioners on Sunday evening and I would remain virtually quiet all evening, while she engaged in conversation with them all. We would attribute it to weariness after preaching, and pass it off by claiming, "It's a good thing she's a talker to make up for me." I would come home from a Classis meeting only to tell her I had never spoken up once! Now that I've stepped back from it all and can be more objective and have the perspective of a whole lifetime of ministry, I have finally gained the freedom and courage to say, "I am an introvert," and not feel inferior or guilty about that.

Perhaps it strikes you as unnecessary to pay attention to my personality style. "After all," you may want to say, "a sense of calling and a passion to preach are far more important." Yet, I am convinced that God's work of forming us for ministry also takes into consideration the personality style that we are. He has made us to be who we are, and our effectiveness in ministry will be shaped by our understanding of that. So while you assess your sense of calling, do also pay some attention to your personality style. Take some of the personality tests and seek the insight from some trusted persons who will be honest with you.

It's interesting how that all came about for me. Increasingly, I became honestly aware of the fact that I would rather quietly study than be out in the crowd mixing with people. I could increasingly recognize that I did not speak up in Classis meetings because I didn't have the self-assurance to believe I had something important enough to share. More and more I put the pieces of the puzzle together in a way that made sense. As a result, I have come to see more clearly than ever that my major personality mark is that I am an introvert. I've read two books about it lately, *Quiet*, by Susan Cain, and *Introverts in the Church*, by Adam McHugh. Both are packed with insight, and I resonated with them so well. Both provided the opportunity to assess and evaluate my past experiences and shed interesting light on who I am and how I function. Both are books I should have read some years before. Because I am an introvert, I value time alone, quiet, by myself and find myself energized by such things. I, therefore, can spend long periods of time in my office studying, planning, writing and feeling good about it. I can go to the library to be alone and plan and find it refreshing (my perch on the fourth floor of the library at a local college was a pleasant and safe place for me).

At the same time, I can recall how tiring it would be for me to go out visiting with parishioners on Sunday evening and have to engage in group conversation all evening. I remember sitting at wedding receptions, etc., with others folks and the evening seemed so long! I could meet with others, either colleagues or others, in group meetings and be the quiet one of the group.

In my work now at the seminary and at the college, I value my time in the office here where it is quiet, I can research, write, and find it rewarding. And I came to realize that my problem is compounded by pastors, some of them rather young, who seem very self-assured, and who can think on their feet in meetings. I found it easy to envy them as the best leaders and wondered why I couldn't function that way. My reading on the subject taught me that those pastors are not necessarily in possession of so much more insight than I have, but it's rather that they have a personality that is more extroverted than mine.

I should not be surprised at that because there is ample evidence that many pastors/preachers are introverts. Sometimes I think it must be the majority of them. We just don't recognize it so quickly. We focus more on those who are charismatic, who can relate to everyone, who are the first to speak up, and do so persuasively. But once I became aware of this matter, I also became aware of how many pastors, and also professors, do show signs of being introverted. They would rather spend long hours in their study, researching, writing sermons, writing other articles, and books. It takes an introvert to have the patience to do that.

But now, the problem for me, and many others, comes in the fact that, as one of the books identified it, we are introverts who are called to serve in an extrovert world. The first time I read that chapter, a light went on in my head! "There is the problem," I said, "and that's why it's so hard." The church expects us to be extroverted pastors—we must get to know everyone, we are to remember names, we preach, we lead meetings, we speak up with advice, and we are always available for anyone at any time. The church rarely thinks about the time we need for study and writing in order to preach and teach. The church seems to want pastors who are engaging in relationships, who are motivators of others, without realizing that to be a pastor/preacher means navigating the world of ideas, which by and large is a world of study, reading, reflecting, and writing. So I was forced into an extrovert world. And then on top of that I was put into denominational leadership at synod, various boards, and committees. As an introvert, I was often out of my element, but not free to admit it, or even identify it to myself. Through all of that I discovered that I could serve well in those extroverted roles but found it very exhausting.

As a protective and defensive measure, I learned certain techniques to help me survive. But I discovered these more by accident than intentionally. My office door would be closed as much as possible; I tried to get to the library for study on Tuesday and Friday afternoons; supper time was quiet at home with no phone calls being returned; Saturday afternoon and evening as well as Monday morning were private time. These were my periods for regrouping.

But I realize now that also explains why I was so tired and fatigued so much of the time, experienced times of depression, and often felt burned out. One of the marks of introversion, in contrast to extroversion, is that introverts find energy draining out of them when they are engaging with crowds, whereas extroverts find that same experience to be energizing. I loved my parishioners, but an afternoon of pastoral calling brought weariness to me.

My oldest son, who has the same thing, has developed some coping mechanism that I probably should have developed too. He takes a couple of days away for "Reading Time". At times it seemed like a luxury to me, but more and more I realize it is a healthy therapeutic habit.

I never took opportunities like that, but my "break time" to the library or the cottage of some friends was somewhat of a pattern like that, though I probably took advantage of them too seldom. Now, in this chapter of life, I have greater freedom to do such things. In my case, now, they take the form of yard work in the summer where I can be alone with my thoughts, use my body, and feel creatively productive and find delight in developing beauty in the yard. In the winter, my model railroad room is the safe haven where I can go to express my creativity, enjoy my aloneness, feel productive, and find the quiet.

It continues to amaze me how God does not demand that a person be an extrovert to be a good preaching/pastor, but calls as many introverts as he does others. However, when he does, those introverts have some extra struggles to live with because the church often wants it otherwise. The church is an extroverted world.

In His Service,
Your Colleague

Thinking About It—

What is your personality style as you understand it?

In what ways is your personality style an asset? A liability?

8

Continued Learning in the Pastorate

DEAR PASTOR,

All of life has been an amazing and very intense school for me. The older I get, the more I realize that. Maybe that's not true for some folks, but I surely hope it's true for you. Woe to the pastor who assumes that learning ceases when seminary is completed. I want these words to help you identify and cherish some of the great things you have learned during the years of your ministry so far.

All that I have been writing here is really an account of things that I have learned or come to realize since I left seminary in 1962. When I first came on staff at the seminary in my retirement in 2002, I was asked to present a public lecture at the seminary entitled "Things I Learned in the Ministry—Which Seminary Couldn't Teach Me." That was quite a significant step, to deliver a lecture like that before my colleagues who didn't really understand why I was here at the seminary. But perhaps the most significant part of it was that it stirred in me the motivation to keep on assessing and reviewing how the ministry had changed me. I've touched on a number of them already in this material, but I think it would be good to cite them here again for a quick review. Let's call this a summary of the things I learned in the ministry.

I have learned more clearly than ever that ministers are privileged people. I told you that at my ordination service, the presiding pastor looked me squarely in the eye and said, "It's a privilege to be a minister of the gospel in the Christian Reformed Church. Don't ever forget that there are many others who would give their right arm for it!" Little did I realize how true that is. To be sure there are times when it is taxing and tough, but before long the awareness swells up again that I stand in a mighty privileged position to be captured by the grace of God, called to be his personal servant, participate with him in his work, live for big purposes, have a front-row seat to what he does in people's lives, watch them grow, to plan worship, and preach the word. I still can't think of a better way to invest my life. Unfortunately, it's far too easy to lose sight of that.

Ministers need a deep sense of calling. I have written elsewhere here about the rather unusual manner in which my sense of calling first became clear to me and then kept on expanding. We still ask seminarians to explain how they arrived at their sense of calling. But it wasn't until partway through my ministry that I really came to grasp how critical that was. When those seasons come when the ministry is demanding, discouraging and weariness develops, our hearts can easily wander, wondering if we should continue, and eagerly looking around at other vocations. I did some of that at times too. But I always came back to those deep down convictions that God has chained me here and would let me go nowhere else. Were I not so sure of that, I might have gone somewhere that I ought not to be.

I learned that ministers need a lot of audacity. I came to identify with that word about halfway through my ministry, because I tend to be rather timid of character, and at times a bit short on self-confidence. But audacity is when you think, say, attempt or expect something that seems far beyond reason. Who am I, after all, to think that God would use little me from Muskegon in significant ways! Who am I that I could actually speak for God? And how amazing to actually say to people and the world, God is a God of grace and he will rebuild you! That's audacious! And how audacious to think that people in my parish would actually look to me for advice, prayer, and acceptance.

I found that pastoral work certainly tests our personal faith. Ministers are always supposed to be persons of faith. But it isn't always that way or quite that easy. The rigors of the schedule, the weariness of the work, and the busyness of the ministry life competes with our devotional life, with our priorities, and quickly wears us down. And we see so much pain, suffering and disappointment in people's lives that we get stuck in our own questions, not only laments, but deep hard questions and doubts. I'm no stranger to that and have written about that elsewhere in this material. I have found my faith tested in the ministry far more than I was ever prepared for.

Along with that is the fact that pastors step into intense anguish and pain. They told us this in pastoral care classes, but it didn't really register. I saw it in my mother with all her chronic health problems, but even then it didn't register the way it should have. But when the counseling office and the sick calls put me in touch with other's pain and suffering, I saw and heard things I never expected to see and hear. And then we find the same stuff in our own personal lives, and our family, and we've had our share of it. I have stood by the side of those who have had even more. I've been in the hospital when the doctor asks me where my pain is on a scale of 1 to 10, and I have to tell him. I didn't know there would be such a scale in the ministry, but there is, and though sometimes it's only a 2 or 3, there are a lot of times when it's 5 or 6 or 7, and even some times when it hit 9 and 10! We borrow the pain that others are feeling by our identification with them.

Ministers need to continually keep on studying and growing. When I graduated from seminary I was relieved and didn't really anticipate returning to the classroom anytime soon, if ever. That's another thing on which I was dead wrong! I soon learned, especially through preaching every week, that good ministry comes from a growing minister, and good preaching comes from a growing preacher. Who was I to think I knew enough to feed others lifelong, and how naive to think that the world and the church would not continually change at a pace I couldn't imagine. So, my experience of feeling depleted in preaching from about years eight through ten led me back to the classroom at Calvin Theological Seminary for a summer course and that opened the door for continued study. Several healthy influences contributed to that. It was good to identify my depletion; I was privileged to have some wise elders who encouraged study, book buying, and later even provided sabbatical time for me. And then I gradually noticed among my colleagues that there is a fork in the road about halfway through one's life of ministry. You can begin to divide pastors into two different categories—those who continue to study and grow and those who don't. The first have greater effectiveness and depth; the latter do not.

Worship and preaching are primary for the pastor. You know that from my ministry, and from what I've written here. It was an intentional decision on my part to prioritize it that way. There are just so many hats a pastor has to wear that without careful prioritization secondary things will clamor for the most attention, and the primary things will be shoved into the background. There is a theological reason for that—if the Word is primary, then its exposition is a lot more important than all those tasks of "running a church," and if the worship service is the time when the whole family is together, a pastor's best efforts must be given there. If an active church is to find all its ministries fruitful and effective, it will need worship on the Lord's Day to be Word centered, Christ honoring, and fully engaging.

Pastors run the risk of joylessness. Maybe this is a surprise, for after all who has greater reasons for joy than a Christian minister? Yet I have observed a good many pastors who are joyless a good bit of the time, and I think I also fell into that hole at times. Our spirits sag, we begin to whine, fatigue saps us, we live with the strain of too much to do, we are caught in the crossfire of too many competing expectations, we get a lot of criticism, we step into a lot of folks' suffering, and generally we take ourselves far too seriously. Consequently, we can't laugh at our foibles. Too bad. We lose our sense of celebration, begin to feel sorry for ourselves, and effectiveness in ministry diminishes.

Pastors have too many hats to wear or tasks to balance. Just think of it—two sermons to write each week (or at least one nowadays!), lessons to plan, meetings to lead, counseling sessions, sick calls, books to read, phone calls to return, children to raise, and a marriage to tend to. And the pastor finds himself caught somewhere between being a servant, an errand boy, a vision caster, a communicator, and a student. I had hoped I'd find some help from others in sorting this out, so I talked to friends, elders, committees, other staff members and they all understood the problem but had no answer. They all counseled me that the solution was not to be found in the advice of others but within myself; not to be found in balancing all these tasks, but rather in taking personal responsibility for prioritizing them. What will matter most, what are my gifts, what can I do as a pastor that no one else can do? It was my responsibility to choose and follow through. That decision was left to me!

Pastors must deal with difficult behavior. I don't know if they told me about this in seminary or not, but I might not have been listening if they had. I assumed all God's children would be good, well-meaning, kind and rewarding to work with. That is not the case. Moses had some pretty cantankerous Hebrews to deal with in the wilderness. Early in my ministry, a retired pastor advised me to remember that Jesus had to cope with some very difficult behavior among his disciples too. When it happens, it's very disillusioning. I expected that kind of behavior from those outside the church, but to see it within the church was very distressing. Our survival and effectiveness in ministry is dependent on our being gracious, patient, and able to look beyond the pain of the moment. And I needed to remind myself that some of them may have thought that I was difficult too!

God is sovereign. I learned that first in catechism class and then in systematic theology in seminary. But that was all cognitive, in my brain. It was through the difficult pastoral and personal experiences in the ministry that I had to come to grips with making it a firm personal viewpoint that was my fall-back position. I encountered so many things I could not understand, and I read about so much in our world that scared me and made no sense, so my hope and strength then came from my tenacity of holding on to my conviction, based on Scripture, that God is sovereign—no matter what! Sometimes I had to talk to myself over and over during the night on that one! God can and will do what he believes should be done for his ultimate purposes. Sometimes that will make sense to me and sometimes not. Either way, he remains God!

The church is Christ's church. He bought it, he called it together, and he will protect it until the end of time so that even the gates of hell cannot prevail against it. If that's true for the church at large, it's also true for Lebanon, Trinity, Bethel, and Hillcrest, the congregations I served. I do my part and try to shape it for a few years, but ultimately it belongs to Christ. None of them ever were "Howie's church." It's so easy to think too highly of ourselves and our ministries. It's far too easy to think the welfare of a given congregation is up to us and our efforts, and to assume that the strength and health of a congregation is a tribute to our fine efforts. Interestingly, I found that praying the Lord's Prayer was a good corrective of that error.

Of course, underneath all of this is the humbling truth that God uses very weak and flawed tools to lead his church. I knew that ahead of time and had no fancies about any superior abilities on my part. I often read 1 Corinthians 1:26–31 to be reminded of it. These are profoundly insightful words:

> Brothers and sisters, think of what you were when you were called. Not many of you were wise by human standards; not many were influential; not many were of noble birth. But God chose the foolish things of the world to shame the wise; God chose the weak things of the world to shame the strong. God chose the lowly things of this world and the despised things—and the things that are not—to nullify the things that are, so that no one may boast before him. It is because of him that you are in Christ Jesus, who has become for us wisdom from God—that is, our righteousness, holiness and

redemption. Therefore, as it is written: "Let the one who boasts boast in the Lord."

My surprise, and my comfort, is that God would use a weak tool like me to do some work that I believe is very good. But that means, of course, when there is any good, all glory goes to him. I sin when I try to take credit for myself.

To say I learned all these truths in the ministry does not mean they all came right away. Learning goes slowly. Sometimes truths as big as these sink in slowly, through pain, and through relearning over and over.

It's been a long time since I entered the ministry, and I'm still learning. I don't know how long you've been in the ministry, but however long it is, I'd suggest you try to make a list of new insights you have gained along the way. Make your list of "things I've learned since leaving seminary" and then share it with someone close to you.

In His Service,
Your Colleague

Thinking About It—

> Make your list of "things I've learned since leaving seminary" and share it with colleagues in the ministry.

> Ask your colleagues to share their list of such things with you.

9

A Pastor for All

Dear Pastor,

It probably wasn't long into your first pastorate before you were struck by the wide range of age and circumstances within your congregation. From infants, to adolescents, to young parents, to mid-lifers, to empty nesters, to senior citizens; from the never married, to widows and widowers, to divorcees. They are all there. The rich and the poor. The healthy and the chronically sick. Are you expected to be the pastor for all of them? Are you supposed to be able to communicate wisely with all of them? Can you possibly do that? Will your time allow you to serve them all? Can you possibly live into and understand the life-needs of each?

And with that realization another quandary of ministry crept into your awareness.

There is an easy assumption that most of us seem to begin with, at least unconsciously. We minister best to those of our own age group and in circumstances similar to ours. Our sermons seem to be written for people our age; our illustrations reflect life among those like us; our friendships in church are with those who are similar in age to us; and in pastoral care we relate best to those closest to us. But what about all the others who notice this and feel left out? Should a pastor be expected to care for all? And how intentional should a pastor be in such matters? Is it possible and fair to expect us to relate to all?

My experiences in four congregations illustrates this quandary rather clearly. I found the ministry to be very demanding, my schedule was full, and my time was in short supply, and yet there were always more people to serve than I was able. When it came to funerals, it was always a given that age was no factor. I was to serve all. From children to grandparents, all were sacred. The fact that my pastorates were marked by a large proportion of young families with small children made it too easy to give little attention to the senior members of the congregation. In the first two pastorates, I was a young man and therefore seemed to naturally gravitate to the youth, young adults and young couples. To make a call on older folks quickly took me out of my comfort zone. As I aged, so did my comfort zone. In middle age, I related to middle-agers best. As I got older, the seniors came to mind more.

And I also began to notice some contradictory factors in the life of my congregations. They brought infants for me to baptize them, but then seemed to assume they were unimportant minors until they grew up. Parents were expected to bring their children to worship, but there were no expectations about the need for me to pay any attention to them in the liturgy. We said the entire church is one unified body, and then separated everyone in classes and study groups according to their age and chapter in life. We developed a staff ministry with a separate staff member in charge of children's ministries and youth ministries and left the senior pastor out of the picture for them. Even cultural practices were confusing. Theoretically we said all persons of whatever age are equally valuable and sacred, but when some of them became old and needy we took them out of the community and put them away in special institutions.

Gradually, fed by some of these anomalies, new influences began to invade our churches and along with them came great impact on our pastoral relationships and faced us with new questions.

- Our pedagogy became much more intentional. It was not enough for a child to sit quietly in worship, nestled next to mother, assuming faith would enter by osmosis. Careful age-related methods were needed to engage them as they grew and the pastor was to be part of that.

- The formation of faith encouraged cross-generational conversations as necessary so that old and young would converse together and share their faith stories. So we asked hard questions about those forms of ministry which separated and isolated people by their age groups.

- While our culture taught us the value and centrality of children, church leaders had to learn not to say that children are the church of the future but the church of now. Instead thinking it was sufficient that children are seen and not heard, they are to be included with integrity. And leaders were to focus their efforts on children in terms of their current faith level.

- Gradually, the church came to affirm the essential value of all generations. No one is to be valued above the others. Children are as valuable as middle-agers; seniors as valuable as adolescents; and no one is to be considered inferior. But that meant, of course, that all ages deserve the same kind of pastoral care and attention.

As a result of these influences, new efforts of ministry soon began to appear in the church, nearly all of which impacted the role of the pastor. How well the pastor related to each age group often influenced the personal effectiveness (or lack of it) of a pastor. Hymnals soon began to include both historic hymns, and also children's songs and choruses. Worship planners were encouraged to make room in the liturgy not only for the sanctuary choir but also a children's choir. Pastors were expected to provide a children's sermon that would be able to speak to them on their level with their vocabulary in an engaging manner. Parents were heard to critique the pastor's sermons on the basis of whether their children got anything out of it or not. At the same time the integrity of a pastor was shaped by the attention given to seniors.

These shifts created many new questions for pastors. Can I possibly minister to the seniors of church while still relating to the youth? Can I stay in touch with the children of the congregation even though I have no formal time with them? Is it possible to be the pastor for all? And then also ask which other group in your congregation needs more attention, such as, singles, divorcees, widow(ers), seekers, etc.

Each pastor must wisely and prayerfully deal with these concerns. Several factors will likely shape our response:

- What are my gifts and abilities? Our understanding of this will focus our attention on our primary duties. The question we'll have to continue to wrestle with, though, deals with how we can continue other forms of service that are expected of us though not particularly in our gift mix.

- What does my job description say? Written or assumed, the duties of each position are normally outlined by the church and this formulation must guide us. This will indicate whether we have been called to be the solo pastor to the entire congregation or to a specific ministry to a limited group.

- How can I learn to provide loving care to those not necessarily in my age group, or in a circumstance of life similar to mine? We are obviously most comfortable with those of like circumstances, but love leads us to often serve outside of our comfort zone.

- Where are the needs the greatest? The heart of a committed pastor moves in the direction where the needs are the greatest, regardless of other factors.

- Remember the model of Christ. He never limited his love because of a comfort zone. Wherever there was human need he provided servant love. We see him with children on his knee, a daughter to be raised, a widow in grief, blind persons, and the poor. He never asked whether they were male or female, Jew or Gentile, young or old. He loved and served all.

In His Service,
Your Colleague

Thinking About It—

> When you write a sermon, or plan a worship service, which age groups do you generally have in mind?

> Which age group—children, adolescents, post-highs, young parents, middle-agers, seniors—do you think would feel most overlooked in your congregation?

> Which other category of people may possibly feel overlooked in your congregation?

10

The Church in My Rearview Mirror

DEAR PASTOR,

It has now been a number of years since I retired from active ministry and more specifically from Hillcrest Church. My view of the church at this stage can be characterized more as a view through the rearview mirror.

I never realized that the adjustment and transition would be as difficult and traumatic as it has been. In another letter I'll be sure to address the matter of letting go when it's time to move on. For now, let me just say that letting go is painful and involves a measure of grieving, grieving which at times can become pretty intense. You've probably experienced some of that if you've left one pastorate to move to another. As your ministry moves on, you are bound to experience it more.

For now, I find myself readily able to say there is much from the pastorate that I miss. It was a rich and satisfying life, in spite of the occasional disappointments. There were so many times and events that I wish could be repeated. To worship with the same congregation every week, to plan and lead worship weekly, to call them "my people," to know their needs and aim to meet them, to watch children grow to youth and embrace their faith, to marry young couples and watch a family develop, to baptize infants and see delighted parents. And so many more joy-producing experiences.

But I'm also distant enough from it all now that I have an objectivity which enables me to critique my own ministry in ways I could not while immersed in it. And so from time to time, particularly when I teach a class or lead a workshop on worship, I find myself admitting that if I were still in the pastorate I would do some things differently than I did at the time. Not only am I more objective to it all now, but, since I left the pastorate and began here at the Institute of Worship and the seminary, I have continued to grow (by leaps and bounds) in my thinking about worship and best worship practices. I wish I had had all this insight back then. I don't aim to be exhaustive here, but I'd like to suggest a few of the "things I'd do differently." Perhaps they will stir some reflections on your part.

I think it would be wise to read more Scripture passages in each worship service. I didn't follow the Revised Common Lectionary in preaching, but I wish I had used it for other Scripture selections. Each service would include multiple readings—OT, Gospel, Psalm, Epistle, for example. If the power of the Spirit is in the Word, then we should always have room for plenty of Scripture readings. I think some of our services were rather sparse in such readings. I did refer to passages, but our people did not receive the diet of balanced passages being read. I know we often wrestle with time issues, and feel that worship services are too full, but it seems to me now that a priority in this struggle should be in the inclusion of more Scripture.

I'd certainly do more to remember our baptisms. Because we practice infant baptism, we have a problem of forgetting it, and our memory of it becomes less and less clear. I know I was baptized as an infant, and it's primarily because of my father's reminders that I kept that in mind. I suspect that for too many such an awareness is lost except way back in the recesses of their memory. Almost every service ought to have a verbal reference to our baptism in Christ. Most of our calls to worship might well include a reference to our baptism as the source of our identity, our obedience, our pardon, our praise, worship, etc. I would include this reference at weddings, funerals and professions of faith. And periodically, certainly at least annually, I'd like to have an "affirmation of our baptism vows." It seems that would be very timely and meaningful as a standard Old Years / New Year's or First Sunday of the New Year event for a congregation. The formation of our faith would surely be enhanced by facing the need for such a reaffirmation at least annually. I would make regular use of the liturgy entitled "Affirming Baptism and Professing Faith." It can be found in the hymnal *Lift Up Your Hearts* and *The Worship Sourcebook*, as well as other places.

I would also work harder to build understanding and rapport with those who disagree with me on matters of worship. Too often we divide into camps around our preferences and opinions and become us-and-them groups. A culture like that usually knows how to function only when they have ideas and proposals that they can debate and argue about to see who wins. It is so easy to separate, withdraw, and harden our opposition to one another and such a situation is not usually very healthy for a congregation. I know that greater dialog would take work because my personality is such that I too easily become defensive, withdraw, and avoid conflict. I'd have to intentionally seek dialog with them to achieve understanding, and be willing to do a lot of intentional listening. It might have avoided some of the conflict that has developed at times.

Along with that, I would double up my efforts to teach about worship and its issues. Looking back, I am conscious of the earthquake that has occurred in worship thinking during the past thirty years. Our congregations were all caught in these conflicts without realizing the setting and context of it all. First, my own study would concentrate on learning about worship issues. I think I'd write a regular column for the congregational newsletter on a variety of issues to teach the congregation. And I'd hold an adult education class perhaps every other year to study the issues with a group.

I would also do things differently with my prayers within a worship service, especially the major pastoral prayer. It would be more "outward looking" and not so exclusively focused on our own local needs. I'd scour the newspapers and news reports for issues of our world that need attention, and I'd even include a small core of people who would do prayer-research for me each week. Then at the beginning of the pastoral prayer I'd take time to point out the needs of our world which need to be part of our intercessions today. I'd want our prayers to be a time when the whole world is held up for God's mercy.

I have previously pointed out that my introverted personality needs more quiet and "away" retreat times for reading, prayer, and study. I tried to accomplish that by a weekly afternoon at the library, but I should have done it more intentionally with specific study times for more than an afternoon. It would have enabled me to leave the stress of the ministry behind on a regular basis. I am confident that I have sufficient self-discipline that I could be sure to use such time well.

There are also times when I reflect on the stance of the congregation vis-à-vis the world and the culture in which we live. The congregations I served saw themselves as a healthy part of their community. They served the community, influenced local events, and wanted to be recognized as a contributing element of community life. I always encouraged that and was very much a part of the community myself. But I have to admit that our awareness of the national and world community received inadequate attention. Oh yes, we prayed for our national leaders, and when there were national and world crises we prayed about it. But I must admit that our awareness of and passionate concern for the issues of justice, race, inequity, poverty, and such issues was limited. No one would ever describe me or my congregations as "activists" and I'm questioning that. With our world- and life-view convictions, and with our concern for the lordship of Christ over all, shouldn't we be more concerned about righteousness than comfort, about impact than security? So the view in my rearview mirror tells me that I should have taught and stirred my congregations to be more passionate about issues of justice and righteousness in all its elements.

Other concerns about the stance of the church call for my attention, too. I wonder if I should have been more courageous and prophetic in warning the church about some of its trends that are unhealthy. One of them is Sabbath observance. I really do hurt when I see the rapidly changing practices of Sabbath observance. I know we probably were too legalistic in the past and fell into the trap of blue-laws about it all, but I feel the pendulum has swung largely to the other extreme today among church people. It is so significant to me because I'm convinced it affects the life of the church, and it reflects a changing view of life and living that has infected our families and communities. We are seeing that when pendulums begin to swing, they swing far. I regret that Sunday evening worship is on the way out. I don't think that's just traditionalism, but rather an appreciation for the Old Testament pattern and a concern for sanctifying the entire day. I'm afraid it's a symptom of bigger things that have happened to the Sabbath. I've read Walter Brueggemann's book on *Sabbath Resistance*, and I was captured by its opening sentence, "For the most part, contemporary Christians pay little attention to the Sabbath." Right on, Walter! I see all this, and I wonder what more I should have said and done.

One of the others is the adoption of a worldly lifestyle that a previous generation was so careful to avoid. Yes, we were too separate as an ethnic community; yes, we had legalistic rules about dancing, card-playing and movie-going (things that now sound rather silly). But we were aware of our status as a minority in society. But today another pendulum is swinging. We attend movies indiscriminately; we watch stuff on TV that is far worse than our parents were concerned about in theatres; drinking and openly referring to it is acceptable everywhere in church communities. I wonder if our budgets were revealed what it would show about the percentage we spend on ourselves and our recreation and what that would say about our stewardship. And then at the same time churches and mission agencies complain about the shortage of funds that are available. And Christian education suffers from lower enrollments because "it's just so expensive today." We seem to have drunk in so thoroughly from a materialistic, narcissistic lifestyle, without any embarrassment at all. And I wonder, should I as a pastor have said more?

Since virtually all of my work is in the field of worship, you can imagine that I watch it very closely. In addition, I preach in quite a variety of churches and get to see all kinds of worship. On the one hand I'm encouraged by the renewed interest in worship, the renewal and vitality of worship, which has given rise to the Institute of Worship. And yet, there are some deep concerns I have. We seem not to be concerned, or even aware, that our children are growing up without an awareness of the Ten Commandments, the Apostles' Creed, and other things that were so familiar to us. I often wonder if such timeless formulations will be in their minds and hearts when they get older and really need it.

And part of that problem is the loss of a sense of history— we're raising a new generation that does not even know some of the historic and classic Christian creeds and hymns. They are not aware of people and issues in our history that have had such a large hand in shaping us. It's the historylessness of it all that bothers me.

There is much for which to give thanks; much to be concerned about. I consider it a privilege to have served the church. And when I look in the mirror I see so much for which to be grateful, but I also see these I have pointed out in which I wish I had handled things differently. I raise them to stimulate your thinking and reflection. God is faithful; it's Christ's church; and the Spirit is still doing his work there.

I hope you never lose that confidence.

In His Service,
Your Colleague

Thinking About It—

> If you had the opportunity to start your ministry over, what would you do differently this time?
>
> Make a list of your greatest concerns for the church today and share it with colleagues. Compare your list with theirs.

11

The Faith Drama

DEAR PASTOR,

Is it OK for me to share with you some of the intense struggles my pastoral heart goes through? Sometimes my feelings are so conflicting that it gets me down. Yet I hesitate to share it with you for fear of giving you undue concern. But then I think that it's not so bad to share it with you, because there probably are times when you are experiencing the same thing. To hide it from you might contribute to your feelings of aloneness at such times. Yet it is a large concern of mine, one that I have never really been able to resolve. I think of it as the "Drama of Faith." And I have come to see that none of us are immune to it—preachers included.

On the one hand, it's the only way to give you a candid and accurate picture of the ministry because our experiences as a pastor often create this kind of stress. All human beings encounter that, but when you are in the Christian ministry you probably will encounter it with even great intensity. You see, life in this world is a mixture of good and bad, of what makes sense and what doesn't. You already know that. So it should come as no surprise that you and I are caught in the middle of the test that creates. I was not surprised that such times came, but I was rather surprised at how difficult it was for me to find a way to resolve them. Indeed, to this day, some of it has never been resolved. It throws me back into the Lord's lap to trust him, and allow him to use me, even when I don't have everything all straightened out in my mind and heart. Some of this does bring up the subject that I am a person who can tend toward mild depression, not severe, but it's there enough that I take notice of it. I'm really not concerned about that, for I've read enough about other leaders and preachers, many of whom seem to be marked by the same tendency.

My confusion is largely caused by the incongruity of how I feel and how I think I *ought* to feel. I have two sets of reactions and they don't seem to match. Let me summarize it all by telling you that I can quickly tend to feel down, isolated, mildly depressed, sad, and tears can be my companion more than I wish they were, and yet I have so much for which I ought to be grateful, encouraged, and deeply satisfied. And on another level, there is so much that I see in the church and in the lives of people that is sad and tragic and makes life seem so heavy. At the same time, I see and experience so many wonderful things and evidences of God's special care that ought to stir joy and thanks. There is a lot that I know about with my head that doesn't seem to register in my emotions, and I'm just not sure how to get the two together. My guess is that if you were to talk to other people near me about these things, they might be very surprised to hear that I have a tough time of it, because I think I'm pretty good at covering it up. I can function normally, engage in up-beat relationships, even while I'm feeling sad. On the one hand, I think that's good because it shows my down time is not interfering with how I function; but on the other hand maybe I'm concealing too much and burying it unhealthily. When I think about those times of covering it up and continuing with ministry, even preaching, I don't feel dishonest. Instead, I see that God through his Spirit intends to equip and use me, even with my struggles, and it's a tribute to his grace that he'll use a broken vessel like me to keep on doing his work. On the other hand, I'm grateful he doesn't tell me that he'll be able to use me for his work only when I get all my struggles resolved.

The things getting me down come from many sources. I hear the evening news and encounter them; I read the newspaper and find them there; I talk with friends about their experiences; as a pastor I step into people's lives and experiences; and I have my own family and their experiences. Life is such a mixture of good and bad, of what makes sense and what doesn't, of times when I am affirmed that I see God at work and when I can't seem to find any trace of his work at all.

Surely you know what I mean. There is so much that just doesn't add up! I see diseases, broken marriages, tragic accidents, death, violence, and war. What I see and what I believe don't match! And that bothers me a lot. Not only does it bother me to be feeling down when those close to me are hurting, but it bothers me that I'm can't seem to quickly balance it out with the good things that are happening around us all the time.

Sometimes (often?) the best sermons come not just from careful study, but from personal struggles, and that's true of one of the sermons I preached recently. Actually I've preached it several times and each time I feel more and more at home with the way it develops, and the struggle it identifies. But after preaching it a few times, I've put it away because the pain I feel in it is just too intense. I've called the sermon *Competing Voices*. It's from Mark 9:24 and is about the father with the demon-possessed son who responds to Jesus by exclaiming, "I believe . . . help me overcome my unbelief." In this sermon I develop the reality that living in this world today (post-Genesis 3) often involves a lot of difficult experiences that make it tough going. And when that happens we are caught between two competing voices—one says "I believe" and one says "but I can't really believe." I won't give you the whole sermon here, but it surely is an autobiographical sermon, more than I realized at the beginning.

I don't know how typical it is of other preachers, but I feel that I really am someone who is caught between competing voices a good bit of the time. I believe that I have a very firm faith, and I trust God no matter what. I never consider giving up on my trust in God, and I mean it genuinely when I tell others they ought to do the same. I can freely talk about things I don't understand, mysteries I face, and yet leave it all in God's hands at the same time.

Yet, I am a person with a tendency to respond with "yes, but . . ." a good bit of the time. I have the strain of skepticism within me. Frankly, I don't know if that's normal or whether I have more of that than others do. But it's always there. And I'm guessing that you may have some of the same thing. After all, if you are a faithful pastor, then you encounter all the evidence of pain and evil that I do, and you must react with the same empathy that I do and the same desire for some resolution that I have, and that it doesn't come very easily for you either. So I'm assuming that you are often caught in this faith-drama as I am. Am I right?

For instance:

-When folks are telling stories and even giving testimonies about how powerful prayer is and how it has changed things or healed someone, my mind immediately wants to think of those instances where it didn't change anything at all, and ask, "What about those?" I want to say, "Yes, but I prayed for other friends and they died!"

-And it seems so much of this stems from my painful experiences in life. (Please don't misunderstand; I'm not saying that I feel my life has been painful, for it has been wonderful and I consider myself to be abnormally blessed; but it's a wonderful life with a fair amount of pain in it.) And it's the pain that makes me ask "why?" I don't really ask it rebelliously, but only from the standpoint of a skeptic, or perhaps as a therapeutic expression of my experience of pain. I know and I trust I'll have the answer to these questions someday, or perhaps they won't matter anymore, but I wonder . . . why did my mother have to live with such debilitating arthritic pain all her life? And why did my daughter die in the womb? And why did I have to deal with cancer multiple times? (I know now some great benefits I've reaped from those experiences, but did it really have to take that?) And why have some dear friends had such heartache with the spiritual development of some of their children and grandchildren? And why have my own children and grandchildren had to undergo some of the painful experiences they've had?

-And my work in the pastorate has not been easy at all, walking through deep times with parishioners. And why did Jon have to die when he had so much to offer at school, church and to his family? And why did Ken get hit with a heart attack when he was such a key person at school and he was so fit physically? And I could go on with a number of others. I just don't understand these things!

-And I look around in our world and in our society. Here's a child killed by a drunk driver! And here are Isaac and Abby, my dear adopted grandchildren, abandoned and mistreated so early in their lives in Haiti that they have so much to get over before they can enter a healthy life. And here are hundreds/thousands of other children who are abused, neglected, caught in poverty, and warfare. And then I want to cry out, "Why, God, why don't you do something about it!?" I find my feelings are so deeply stirred by such things.

Please understand that I am not railing at God, not telling him he did the wrong thing. And I'm not claiming that God is not in control, and certainly am not making claims that I can't trust him anymore. Or am I? Do I sound that way? I do love him, and I do trust him, and I always fall back on that. But I wonder . . . why does he allow all these tough things to happen?

Before I entered the pastoral ministry I never encountered struggles like this. Or maybe I just didn't allow myself to face them. But once I entered this life of service to Christ and his people it all came crashing in. I regularly encountered pain among God's people, and such pain regularly brought up questions about it all, and only some of the time could I find answers. And when answers were absent the drama of faith began.

It was at that point that I came to understand and value the passages of lament, particularly in the Psalms. I was comforted to find those laments for when I voiced my earthy grunts and complaints to God, and when I raised my voice in frustration and accusation, I tended to feel very guilty. But if there is guilt with being that honest with God, why did the Psalmist have the right to do so, and why would they be recorded in Holy Scripture? (Think of Pss 10, 13, 42–43, and 88.) Is it not true, instead, that such laments are normal for God's people on this earth, and that God understands the drama of faith that we all, but especially pastors, experience and that he gives us the right to be honest with him, to cry out our laments? And then it must be true that he is reassuring us that he can handle the laments, the cries, and the pain of the drama of faith.

I know now that from time to time I have to go back to the closing chapters of Job. After Job's friends tried to help, and instead only complicated things, God begins to confront Job with all the evidence of his sovereignty, power, wisdom, in contrast to Job's insignificance, smallness, and weakness. And finally Job responds as he should, and says to God,

> I am unworthy—how can I reply to you? I put my hand over my mouth. I spoke once, but I have no answer— twice, but I will say no more. . . . I know that you can do all things; no plan of yours can be thwarted. . . . Surely I spoke of things I did not understand, things too wonderful for me to know. . . . My ears had heard of you but now my eyes have seen you. Therefore I despise myself and repent in dust and ashes. (from Job 40 and 42)

I know that when I consider what Job experienced there, and then add to it the message of the gospel that Christ came, died, arose from the dead and went back to heaven, I have every reason to say, "OK, I'll live with my questions and mysteries, refuse to be dragged down by them, and I will trust the might, power, and grace of God as the one who knows, and supervises all things wisely! Yes, I can trust him . . . even with my questions! And I arrive at a point of doing that so well, but I wish it would just stick! And it does for a while, but then I slip off again."

I remember how Lew Smedes wrote in one of his books (*How Can It Be All Right When Everything Is All Wrong?*) that the hardest believing there is, real and deep believing, is believing against the grain. When everything around us seems to shout "no, no, no," we still trust God and go ahead without any answers.

I have. And I will. But sometimes it is surely not so easy! Interesting, how we who preach to others are often busy speaking to ourselves too. So in your ministry experiences, I am sure that you will experience some of the same. I've shared my heart with you so that when those times come, you will not feel alone. I encourage you to be honest with yourself about the drama of faith in your own heart, and to find another Christian whom you trust and with whom you can confide from time to time.

In His Service,
Your Colleague

Thinking About It—

> Have you experienced the "competing voices" spoken about in this chapter? How and when?

> What has been helpful to you in resolving this drama?

12

Surprising People Who Shaped Me

DEAR PASTOR,

I'm sure that when you entered the Christian ministry your intentions were like mine—to shape others. In our more grand moments we had thoughts of shaping the church, or at least our own congregation. But when realism entered, our hopes focused more on shaping some other people to be more like God wants them to be. I'm sure we are all confident we have done a good bit of that, perhaps not as much as we desired, but substantial nonetheless.

But the other side of it, to which we probably didn't give a lot of thought, was that God would also send certain key people along who would shape us. And there were many in my life and ministry. I'm sure there are in yours too and I hope you are able to gratefully identify them.

The list for all of us can surely be long, and it may be difficult to select the primary shapers. For me, my parents obviously had a large hand in that. So did my dear wife, Ellie. And many key friends. But certain parishioners had a large hand in it too. There were many, too many to recall or to cite here. But as I reminisce on forty years of ministry there are certain people who stand out. I cite some of them here, though the hardest part of this is to narrow it down to a small number. I'll mention just a handful of them here in the hopes these thoughts will cause you to identify persons like this in your ministry, or to look for them soon.

Peter

The one who perhaps more than anyone else has shaped me, both personally and professionally, has been my uncle Peter H. Elder-sveld. "Uncle Peter" was a younger brother of my mother who became very well known and respected as the radio minister of the Christian Reformed Church on the Back to God Hour. His life was not a long one but it was an extraordinarily influential life. He was such a prominent leader in his day that it seems a shame today when I ask so many others if they remember him, that very few do. That's how easily even prominent leaders are forgotten by the next generation.

Two things bring him to my remembrance now again. I occasionally read some of his sermons along with my morning devotions, such as *Getting the Right Pitch*, his first book, and *The Word of the Cross*, the one that lays out his convictions about the importance and power of preaching. Stimulated by these, I've gone back to skim through my ThM thesis, "A Voice for the Historic Christian Faith," an extensive study and analysis of his ministry, convictions, radio sermons, and his influence in the church. Reading this material brings it all back, and I realize that he has been an inordinate influence in my life.

Peter graduated from Calvin College and went to Calvin Seminary, graduating in 1937, and became a candidate for the Christian ministry. His first pastorate was the Christian Reformed Church of Holland, Iowa. After that he served the Bethany Church of South Holland, Illinois for a few years and then the denomination called him to be the denominational radio minister in 1947. Our family, especially my parents, always considered him to be the key influential person of our family circle. His brothers and sisters, though becoming successful academically and professionally, never were very strong spiritually, and so my mother and Peter had a lot in common as the two spiritually matured ones.

I had the privilege of seeing him in a different role in our family gatherings where casual and more personal conversations always took place. I was delighted to "listen in." Since I was always "going to be a preacher" from the fourth grade onward, I think Uncle Peter took special interest in me, encouraging me along the way, telling me to be a "good one," involving me in some of the family conversations about the church, and even being willing to come to Lebanon, Iowa, to preach for my ordination service. His words and challenge were unforgettable. You might recall my telling the story that a few months after my ordination I was hospitalized for hemorrhaging ulcers and he wrote a letter to me in which he said he was sure I would be distressed by this experience, but I should remember that "no one is really ready to be a good pastor until you have laid between those two white sheets yourself." I have always remembered that, thought of it often, and quoted it to many. Two years later I was stunned by a phone call from Dad that Uncle Peter had passed away from a severe heart attack. I was shocked, and Ellie and I immediately made plans to go to Chicago (Roseland) to be with my family for the visitation and the funeral. It was a special time to hear the reflections of many church leaders and to spend time over the weekend with Aunt Harriett (his widow) in her home.

Little did I know at that time that his influence on me would lead to several other experiences I never would have expected. First, I naturally became the "collector" of the remembrances of Uncle Peter. I put forth effort to get all his books, to retain a file of all his radio sermon booklets, and Aunt Harriett even gave me access to his library, to keep what I wanted, and to prepare the rest for sale or donation. In addition, she gave me some files of his that included some typed manuscripts of other sermons and speeches, including a few tapes. I still have all these materials, and after I'm gone I expect that Heritage Hall will receive them. Second, Aunt Harriett eventually became a parishioner of mine at Bethel Church in Lansing, Illinois. She had been a member of Third Roseland Church, and by the time it closed, I had moved to Lansing, Illinois, and she joined there so I could not only minister to her but enjoy very warm aunt-nephew relationships. My membership on the Back to God Hour Board gave us even more to reflect on together. Our relationship was stretched over several levels—I was a colleague since she always shared ministry with Uncle Pete, so now we could talk about it together; I was a favorite nephew; but in a certain sense I had a bit of a mother/son relationship with her. It was a privilege to officiate at her funeral on January 18, 2001, at Bethel Church. And, third, when I was working on my masters of theology degree at Calvin Seminary and was getting ready to write my thesis, it seemed natural for me to write a review and evaluation of the major themes of his ministry and radio sermons. I did and found it fascinating. Consequently it's a thesis that is larger than they normally are. *A Voice for the Historic Christian Faith* examines his preparation for ministry, his views of preaching, the church he represented, the world in which he ministered, and the major themes of his radio sermons. I read every one of them, and have them all catalogued in the thesis by date and by text.

It was a sad and tragic event when he died so suddenly on October 14, 1965. He was only fifty-four years old, having had barely twenty-seven years in the ministry, and about twenty years as radio minister. I am struck by that, because as I write this I am many years older than he was at his death. That makes me very grateful for the years God has given me; but it also makes me reflect on the fact that, if he had become so prominent and had influenced the church and its mission so thoroughly in those short years, imagine what he could have accomplished if he had lived as long as I have. I know God is all-wise, and that God has a plan, and I can trust him thoroughly, but, wow, those are the kinds of circumstances that make skepticism rumble around within me at times and ask, "Did God really think that one through to take Peter that early, right at the peak of his ministry?"

I shall always be "Uncle Peter's nephew" and when it happens that someone says, "You know, I can hear your uncle Peter when you preach," I feel very complimented. God used him so strategically to shape me into who I am.

Bill

One day, while I was serving in my first pastorate in Lebanon, Iowa, I had a phone call from an elder at Trinity Church in Jenison. He introduced himself as Bill, an elder at Trinity, Jenison, and said, "We're looking for a new pastor and we'd like you to come for an interview with us." I had never heard of him, and I really wasn't considering leaving Lebanon yet. So I respectfully declined, but he said he probably would be calling me back someday. Well, about six months passed and he did call back and I did agree to come for an interview, and that began a years-long friendship with him and his wife, which would significantly shape me. It was the way in which God drew into my life and friendships a man of God who could teach me so much.

The facts are these—I went to Jenison for an interview, loved the church, got the call to become their pastor, accepted it with great excitement, and began my ministry there in April 1966. Bill was vice president of the consistory at that time and took me under his wing to "mentor" me. We became great friends and shared much over the years. Bill was far more important of a fellow than I realized. He worked for Hekman Biscuit Co., had invented Pop-Tarts and designed a marketing plan for them with Kellogg's, and eventually they became very popular. That made him a very important man in the Keebler Baking Company and so in a couple of years he moved to their corporate offices in Chicago. That was our loss in Trinity Church, but our friendship continued. He was generous to us and we would visit them from time to time. Bill became a very influential, powerful corporate man, traveling the world for Keebler, and becoming very wealthy. But Bill (and Floss, his wife) never forgot their roots. They would return to Jenison regularly, not to see prominent people, but to visit the widows, widowers, and the down-and-outers. By doing so he taught me much. I learned that leadership and its influence comes out of love and commitment, not power or authority. I saw that humility is the best virtue, no matter how successful you may be in other things. It was obvious that material possessions are always secondary, and even though he must have become very wealthy, you wouldn't know it. For Bill, service to the kingdom is the purpose and calling we all have in life. And he illustrated that being able to encourage others brings great joy. And, sometimes surprisingly, he was always able to see good in others, good intentions or gifts, and cautioned us all that we not overlook such things. But above all Bill had an infectious personal faith in Jesus Christ, and a constant readiness to share it. Bill was not bound to denominations, and so he could move from one denomination to another as he moved. He moved away from our denomination in later years, in large part, I think, because he became impatient and disappointed with what he considered to be introversion and pettiness in the church.

Mae

Some time ago I made a pastoral call on Mae because she had just had a heart catheterization in preparation for surgery to replace a heart valve. In the process, they discovered several blockages so stents would have to be inserted first. Mae was ninety years old, so this was a big step, one that makes her even wonder if the surgery is wise, given her age. I like Mae. She's a very pleasant person and easy to relate to, a very devout Christian lady, devoted to her children and grandchildren. But my bond with Mae goes even deeper because over the years we have shared together just about every major experience a life can involve. During that afternoon visit, while talking about her surgery, she admitted it probably would be wise for her to write down some of her ideas for her funeral. I encouraged her to do so, and then she asked if I would officiate at her funeral. I agreed, of course. And then we began reminiscing about all the major things we've experienced together. It's quite a catalog of pastor/parishioner/friend relationship.

In 1962, when I arrived at Trinity Church in Jenison, as pastor, I was told a man from the congregation—Mae's husband—was dying of cancer and he needed to meet me. Tom was forty-three years old, father of four children, with advanced lung cancer, who was enduring a great deal of suffering. I got to know Tom and Mae very well through the process of caring for him and spent a lot of time with him in the hospital and at home while bedridden. I had arrived late March, my pastoral relationship with him quickly turned into a friend relationship, but that lasted only a few months, since he passed away in late June. Mae became a young widow at forty-three.

As a follow-up, I regularly visited her as a single mom, got to know her children well, and valued them highly. (At one point I even bought a camper from her!) In the process and over a period of time I heard the professions of faith of her children. I officiated at the marriage of two of them, baptized two of her grandchildren, and even officiated at the wedding of a couple of them. During those years, she and Gary, a widower, decided to marry and asked me to marry them. Mae, a widow, and Gary, a widower, had known each other for years. I married them in our home, the parsonage, in 1971 with all the children of both families present. What was unique about this wedding is that I had arranged the wedding ceremony in such a way that both groups of children also took vows to accept the others into a blended family. Mae's children took vows to accept Gary as a stepfather; Gary's children did the same about taking Mae as a stepmother. And the two groups of children took vows to accept each other. Years later, at Mae's funeral, they fondly recalled that event.

By the time I left my pastorate in Lansing, Illinois, and moved to Hillcrest in Hudsonville, Michigan, Gary and Mae were living in Hudsonville, and they, with their daughter and son-in-law and two grandsons were members of Hillcrest so our paths crossed again. During that time, their need for pastoral care grew because of health problems Gary had. His arthritis was so severe that he was invalided most of the time at home. I called on him regularly. After I retired from Hillcrest, at the time of Gary's death in 2002, I had the opportunity to conduct the funeral—the death of a second husband for Mae! Since that time, I have officiated at Mae's funeral, making the circle very complete. Reflections like these are very valuable for it illustrates how in the Christian ministry we are privileged to meet some wonderful Christian people on a deeper level; not only to meet them but to participate with them on the deepest level of the major joys and traumas of life, stirring their hope and giving them stability in times of pain. As a result, I'm not just a pastor to this family, I'm virtually a member of the family. The church is made up of deeply committed stable people like this! In Philippians 1:3, Paul said, "I thank my God every time I remember you." I do that for Mae and her family. So as friends and parishioners, our relationships have epitomized all that "pastoring" involves in all chapters of life.

Jon

Further reflections on the unique and deepest of my pastoral experiences brings me to a young man who was a friend, and almost a son. Jon will forever be etched in my heart as a true brother and someone whom I had hoped might someday even be a colleague and join me on the church staff. Jon was a teacher at Unity Christian High School in Hudsonville. He taught Bible and ethics, and coached. He was a role model for the students, an outspoken and warmly Christian man. His wife, Barb, and their three children, Ben, Katy and Daniel, were dear friends. While coaching at a spring track meet, Jon developed a stomachache, and came home with what he thought must be the flu. It developed in intensity, and medical care was sought. On Mother's Day, 1994, it was diagnosed as pancreatic cancer in such a location that surgery seemed impossible. Jon was thirty-seven years old. They were devastated, and the entire community (church and school) joined in their feelings of shock and concern. As it turned out, he had only from May into September to live. The cancer was very aggressive, not very responsive to chemo, and caused intense pain most of the time.

What stands out in this experience for me are several factors—how fast it progressed, how much pain Jon had to endure, how absolutely caring and patient Barb could be, and how open and candid Jon was with me. I spent a lot of time with him while in the hospital and at home, toward the final weeks it was nearly daily. Jon was an open book, freely sharing how he felt, his fears, his faith, and his struggle to keep his faith intact. He would read Psalm 88 at night, and wondered if that was OK because it's the only lament without any resolution or hope coming through, but it was how he felt. His struggles made me understand the depth of Mark 9:24, "I believe, help my unbelief!" I gained a far better grasp of lament. But I also gained a better grasp of the therapy that hymns can provide. He had CDs playing softly by his bedside constantly to sooth his spirit. His favorite was "Holy God, We Praise Your Name," a song that will forever be remembered as "Jon's song" in my mind. He had a wish to hear the congregation sing it one more time (as only Hillcrest could sing that song!) before he died. He could attend church no longer, but we had arranged signals that on some Sunday evening when he had a bit more strength, Barb would take him, they would slip into the narthex at the last of the service, and with hand signals I would recognize them, and explain to the congregation (spontaneously!?) that we needed to sing one more song tonight—all his friends knew the story and the plan. We sang it and we cried it . . . and I'll never be able to sing it the same again!

Jon's suffering had perhaps caused me to ask my "whys?" of God more vigorously than ever before. It brought out the latent skeptic in me. For weeks/months I lived with "if God loves us so much and if all these promises are true, then why is Jon not delivered from all this!!??" I must confess that I still wrestle with such "unbelief" at times. My pastoral calls on Jon and Barb were so difficult that I came away from them exhausted and confused. I could cry most of the way home from the hospital. I knew I had to develop some method of self-care, and so I developed a plan with Christy (my secretary) that I would journal my candid thoughts by dictation on the way back to Hudsonville; she would type them out. I still have a sizable "Jon's Journal" in my file drawer. I was careful to have open conversations with Christy so that if it got too heavy or painful she could terminate the work. She's a strong person and saw it all the way through.

Our director of music and I met together with Jon to plan his funeral—the only time we've ever done something like that jointly.

At Jon's funeral, on September 20, 1994, the church was packed with standing room only. The love for him was strongly evident; the solidarity with Barb and the children was strong; and the pain at such an early death was palpable. My message was based on 2 Timothy 4:6–8, a passage of Jon's own choosing.

John and Alyce

While reflecting on all the pastoral involvement I've had and how that gives one a front-row seat in the drama of so many lives, my mind is stirred to many other experiences in the pastorate—some beautiful, some painful, some both. The story of Alyce and John is one I will never forget because it was both pain and beauty of an entirely different kind, the kind I never expected to have and for which my seminary training never prepared me. Alyce and John were a rather quiet, certainly blue-collar family in the congregation, obviously very conservative and traditional. They had four children, all but one had grown, married, moved to another congregation. Alyce came to me one day, in her sixties by then, very embarrassed, to say that John had fallen in love with a much younger lady in the community. He had been running away with her for several days at a time. Alyce was such a pious and conservative lady she could hardly get herself to mention these things. One Saturday afternoon she called to tell me that John was back, and was planning to leave again, and right now was working in his workshop in the back of the house and if I wanted to talk to him that would be an ideal time. I immediately went over there and found John willing to talk to me. He was quite open about his intent to leave soon with his friend to South Carolina for another trip. After talking to him for a while, he pounded his fist on the workbench, "I need that woman's body; I need her body." As I watched, the irony of it all struck me, for his fist was coming down on the bench for emphasis, but every time it came down it landed on a copy of the very conservative journal within our circles. John could not be talked out of it. He went. About a week later an elder and I found (cornered) him with her in a local motel as soon as they returned to town. In short, he and Alyce were divorced; he married the girl who must have been about thirty years his junior; it was a very stormy relationship; and John was soon diagnosed with emphysema. After many attempted conversations by the elders, John was excommunicated from the church. One day the young lady committed suicide on M-45 by running her motorcycle into a truck.

After some time, John was willing to enter conversations again, fostered by a brother-in-law who was a retired pastor, and John appeared for conversation with the elders to make a confession of sin. He was eventually reinstated in membership in the church through reaffirmation of faith, and in 1986 he and Alyce sought remarriage. John knew he had only a short while to live, and Alyce knew "it was the right thing to do." I married them in their son's home in August of 1986. He was sixty-nine; she sixty-seven. Two months later, in September of that year, John passed away, and I conducted his funeral—an excommunication, readmission, remarriage, and funeral for the same person! And all in a short period of years! I am convinced he was sincerely broken, found the grace of God, and I could mediate that grace to him. Alyce died in 2009 and I officiated at her funeral too.

I don't think she ever regretted what she did in accepting John back. She knew "it was the right thing to do." I do not know if the spirit of her heart was really in it or not. I often wonder what the church really thought about all of that. There was no controversy; no real rejoicing; just quiet, with sorrow, with relief, about doing the right thing but finding it all so very heavy. So did I. But at Alyce's funeral I did say I had seen the striking grace of God through her. She had mediated God's grace to John in his dying days and had modeled that grace before all of us.

To be sure, this list is too short. My wife, children, and extended family are a large part of this. And there are so many more who, in smaller or larger ways, pleasantly or in conflict, have shaped me. I am not conscious of many of them, but the message is very clear—God forms us to be who we are through other people with whom we are in relationship.

I encourage you, now and in your ministries in the years ahead, to keep in your grateful heart a list of people who have in the plan of God been your shapers. They will be many. Recognize them as God's special gift to you. Give thanks for them regularly. And make sure they also know how grateful you are for them. They are God's special people in our congregations.

In His Service,
Your Colleague

Thinking About It—

> Make a list of the people whom God has used to be your "shapers"; identify why each one was so significant; share your list with a few colleagues, being careful to protect their identity.
>
> Ask your colleagues to share some "shapers" from their ministry.

13

My Favorite Scriptures

DEAR PASTOR,

From time to time people will ask "so what's your favorite Scripture passage?" I usually asked that of youth when they were making profession of faith, and I did so to find out just how personal their familiarity with Scripture really was. But when people ask that of me, I found it hard to answer because the passage I would point to would change from one experience to another. So I think I'll try to answer it here by calling them "some of my favorite passages through the years." And you'll find that my selections change on the basis of what I am experiencing at that particular time. What is my favorite today might well be replaced tomorrow.

As I write these today, I wonder about you and your favorites. Perhaps you have been preaching the Scriptures for a long time, or just a short while. But as you do, which ones have become most deeply personalized for you?

Psalm 34:4

Psalm 34:4, "I sought the Lord, and he answered me; he delivered me from all my fears." This one stood out for a long time, beginning with my first cancer encounter in 1972. It was at that time that my wife and I discovered Psalm 34. I think there are several reasons why that meant so much. That experience with cancer was really the first time in my life that I experienced deep fear—fear of cancer, fear of what the treatment process would involve, and the fear of an early death. David's experience of fear made me feel at home with him; his ability to be candid about it gave me freedom to do so and to realize that it's OK for Christians to admit they have fear. But even more was the testimony that he brought it to God and the Lord answered him. In v. 6 the Lord helped him with his troubles, but in v. 4 (first!) the Lord helped him with his fear. I found strength and hope in that. I hung on to it personally, and shared it with many others in hospital calls. I'm sure many of them have considered it a favorite since that time. It gives them permission to be honest about their struggles and know that Christ does not rebuke them for it or reprimand them to believe more.

Romans 8

Romans 8, actually the whole chapter, is another one. I found myself landing on different parts of it at different times, but no chapter has been more precious than this one. It is packed with promises, stability, assurance, and security. From "no condemnation" to "heirs of God" to the "Spirit intercedes for us" to "God works for the good of those who love him" to "more than conquerors" and finally to "nothing shall separate us," I came to realize that I would never really uncover all the richness of this great chapter. So this chapter has accompanied me into many hospital rooms to be shared with Christians who are having a tough time of it on their journey.

I have written and preached series of sermons on this chapter, but after I had finished it, I still felt as though there is still more that I have not yet uncovered.

Mark 9:24

Still another is the exclamation of the father in Mark 9:24, "I do believe; help me overcome my unbelief." I have written elsewhere in these reflections (see ch. 9) how I have a bit of the skeptic in me. Sometimes I find it hard to accept things at face value with a quick statement that "God can do anything" because I immediately want to ask, "Then, why didn't he do such and such?" I think all of us probably have a certain strain of this, but I am able to identify it and admit it. So I am conscious of how I have belief and unbelief side by side as competing voices within me. So this father in Mark 9 is a fellow with whom I feel right at home. He's honest about the struggle he has, but never gives up his faith. And Jesus accepts him, does not rebuke him, but proceeds to heal the son and thereby affirms the father's faith. I find it so encouraging and comforting that Jesus does not rebuke him. It gives me permission to admit my fears and concerns to God without the anxiety of being rebuked for them. It also helps me understand myself when I hear that this father had both belief and unbelief side by side within him. I must admit that I often do too, but wonder if I may be free to address God about this push-pull that goes on in my heart.

2 Samuel 7:18

When David becomes king of Israel and the ark is brought to Jerusalem, David lifts his heart in prayer and the first words are, "Who am I, Sovereign Lord, and what is my family, that you have brought me this far?" By divine grace a little shepherd boy, youngest in the family, becomes the king who knows he is in a privileged position in the plan of God. His sense of humility and profound awareness of the surprise God frequently springs on people is something I can identify with. I often resonate with that—that by divine grace a timid little blond boy, son of an immigrant factory worker, is put in the privileged position of the Christian ministry, serving great churches, and a denominational leader, with a family that is exemplary. The surprise of grace and providence of God working together! I'm grateful for such a combination of care and surprise. The care makes me feel very secure. The surprise puts the emotion behind the thanks that I feel.

Psalm 8

There's a surprise in Psalm 8 that causes David to cry out "how majestic is your name in all the earth!" The heavens and all the earth are the product of God's creative power for he has set it all in place. That's all so magnificent! But then it seems so incongruous that God should pay attention to little humans like us. But he does! I love creation; our vacation trips have normally been focused on seeing the beauty of creation, my work in the yard is an act of immersing myself in creation, and I even wish I had studied astronomy more to see the vastness of it. And then in the context of all of that I'm thrilled to think that this sovereign and powerful God has paid attention to us humans, even me, and even to the extent of charting out our lives and sending his Son for our salvation. The anomaly of it all is that the God who creates mountains and manages the sun, moon, and stars has time and attention for little people like me. And he not only pays attention to us but calls us "a little lower than the heavenly beings" and declares that we are crowned with glory and honor. Wow! How magnificent is his Name!

1 Corinthians 15:20

Paul writes, "But Christ has indeed been raised from the dead, the first fruits of those who have fallen asleep." There was a time, early in my ministry, that I struggled with a big question I could admit to no one else. I was haunted at times with the fear that maybe this whole thing of the Christian faith was a hoax, sincerely taught to us by parents, churches, teachers, etc., who meant well, but were sincerely mistaken. Wouldn't it be terrible (I mean, full of terror) to discover (someday when it's too late) that it's all false?

That struggle ended when I read this chapter carefully and realized that the key to it all is the resurrection of Christ. It is sure . . . he did arise . . . there is proof of it in the Bible and in all his appearances. And that sets Christianity apart from all other religions. Other religions are built on the teachings of a man they call important; the Christian faith is built on the actual death and resurrection of Jesus Christ who is identified as the Son of God! My faith is built on the supernatural resurrection of its leader! It is sure and I am safe and I am a "first fruit" who will experience the same thing!

I'm grateful that after digging into the powerful assurance of that text, my struggle with skepticism disappeared!

Obviously, this list is far too short. From the hundreds and hundreds of special truths, promises, and affirmations in the Bible, this is a very small slice. As I review what I have written and the favorites I have selected, I am struck at how the theme of "being surprised" is the common thread through most of them. Yes, I am a surprised pastor—surprised at God's grace, God's care, God's good work, and how God uses vessels like us!

You also will find so many which match the spirit of your heart at just the right time. What are they? Wouldn't it be fascinating and inspiring for us to get together and put together a composite list of all our "Favorite Scriptures"?

In His Service,
Your Colleague

Thinking About It—

> Do that with your colleagues—put together a composite list of all your "Favorite Scriptures." Be sure you explain why they have become favorites.

> Now consider doing the same thing with your family members.

14

Surprises That Come Our Way

Dear Pastor,

In 1962 I entered the ordained ministry with a great deal of eagerness. Can you identify the feelings you had when you entered your life of ministry? My eagerness was fueled somewhat by the fact that I felt very ready to get away from the classroom. After all, I had been in the classroom for nineteen years of my life. It was time to enter my life's vocation. I couldn't imagine remaining in the classroom for further study (that desire was to come later). So I began my first pastorate with great eagerness. I was sure this would be an exhilarating and inspiring career.

But I soon discovered that surprises were in store for me. The ministry was certainly as exhilarating and exciting as I anticipated. But it was also filled with surprises that I never anticipated. Some of them were very painful and reminded me that I would be called upon to die with Christ in this calling. Perhaps you are experiencing some of those right now and if so, perhaps identifying them will give you encouragement. Others were difficult because they provided insight into myself, calling on me to learn things about myself that I had not previously discovered. Still others came as a surprise because of how complex and difficult the gospel ministry is. Yet other surprises were very pleasant and thrilling as I saw how

God was planning to use me to accomplish his work in the lives of others.

One of the first that I encountered was to learn how difficult it was to preach well. I looked forward to preaching. I had been told it was a beautiful task and a high calling. But two sermons a week became very demanding. With little time for breaks and vacation, I had to write and preach between seventy-five and ninety sermons a year. And I arrived at my new pastorate with barely twenty sermons that I owned. I was weary after Sunday so I relaxed on Monday and then the fright of it hit me on Tuesday: what can I find to write sermons on for this week again? I tried to do some experimenting with different styles of sermon-writing, but Sunday just kept on coming more rapidly every week. When I moved to my second pastorate after nearly four years, I assumed that now it would be easier. "I have a file of sermons to fall back on," I mused. But when I tried that, pulling out a sermon or two I had used several years before, I was severely disappointed with its quality and wondered which I should do first—write a new sermon, or write a letter of apology to my former pastorate! I tried new approaches, read books about preaching, went to preaching conferences, and even began taking some summer courses at the seminary. But I found that learning to preach well would haunt me all my life. I was sure that by the time I'd preached for ten years I could assume I had it pretty well figured out. Not so. Not even after twenty years. I was surprised at how difficult the task really is. I loved it, but I was haunted by how difficult it is.

Another surprise came to me in the form of discovering how deeply into the lives of my parishioners I would be invited to go. I have mentioned previously that the gospel ministry gives us a front-row seat in the lives of many people. When I read the Bible, I learned about the good things God was doing in the lives of people—of Moses, of David, of Jonah, of Matthew, of Paul, and Lydia, and so many others. All those stories made the Bible a very living and fascinating book. But as a young man, growing up in Muskegon, I looked around me in my home church, and only rarely did I catch a glimpse of God doing big things like this. Most of their stories just seemed very ordinary. But when I entered my first pastorate, things began to happen and I could see it. I could see it because my seat was a front row seat now. I saw children born and come to know the Lord; couples marry and establish a Christian home; diseases striking and people meeting it with a firm faith; tragedy entered and people found they could cope with it; youth launched into life with a firm profession of faith; others faced death and found peace. I became surprised at all I was able to see and share. I came to realize that the local church is a continually striking drama unfolding. I was surprised to see there was so much more to the local church than meets the eye. And I also came to realize that the pastor gets to see more of it than anyone else. Pastors are welcomed into the inner places of people's lives. He enters the deep places of their being, places where they struggle, pray, doubt, argue with God, resist God, submit to God, learn to repent, and find new faith. I had looked forward to pastoral care as a rich dimension of ministry, but little did I know how deep pastoral care can become. Not only was I surprised to enter those lives so deeply, but also at how willingly many of them took me in. Yes, some resisted it and kept their privacy, but others opened up and let me see and hear just about everything, sometimes more than I was ready for. It all gave me a whole new understanding of the drama of the Christian life. Learning to live for Christ, coping with life's struggles, handling doubts that come, being honest about failures, and wrestling with God along the way are all there every week in the people of the congregation I call "mine."

All that, of course, involves much more information to process and hold. It also involves secrets that may never be shared. I live with more information about more people than I ever anticipated I would have. The obligation to practice confidentiality is a large one and one which, if violated, could do inestimable damage. So I learned of sin and failure, disobedience and broken promises, doubts and lies, addictions and habits, broken relationships and just about everything else. And yet I had the mysterious task of calling them "God's people," loving them, and standing before them each Sunday with a word from the Lord, a prayer for blessing, a word of rebuke, and a benediction. I learned, through it all that I must learn to love them like their Savior does.

But, as you can imagine, I gradually became surprised at the degree of pain I lived with. I knew there would be pleasure and joy. I had been told that. I saw that in the pastors of my youth. Pleasure and joy were givens, I thought. But when I was called and sent to these folks who made up Christ's church, I also took on much of their pain. There is a lot of pain in the local congregation. It's pain over unanswered prayers, tragic deaths, and disappointments in life. It's pain that comes from children's rebellion, the sudden death of a spouse, of mental illness, loneliness, and scores of other things. I suppose I could avoid them, or when I visit them still remain on the periphery of their pain, and therefore protect myself from such pain. But our Savior didn't do that. He entered right into all our pain and loved us from the inside and he calls us to do the same. The pain in my own life, from the death of a stillborn daughter to three encounters with cancer, I'm sure, has heightened my sensitivity to pain. I recognize it quickly, step into it more easily, feel it more deeply, and will carry it with me for the extent of my life. That, I believe, is what an undershepherd is expected to do. And much of this pain cannot be shrugged off, not if you are a genuine pastor. So it will stay with you, will be your companion during the hours of the night, and your constant companion through the day. That has made me aware of the fact that pastors need to be emotionally healthy and stable. They need to be able to carry pain without being crushed by it, able to feel the pain of others but not own it as their own, and able to see the hurt in others but not become depressed. Of course that means that pastors must make peace with their own tears. One cannot carry such pain from others and remain stoic. Neither can one who breaks down easily lead others well. We each need to find our own balance, and we need to develop our own method of processing their pain.

Perhaps it's because of such things, that another surprise in the ministry involves the degree of weariness you feel. I don't only mean a weary body. That's what happens to all of us. But I mean a weariness of spirit which is harder to resolve. In 2 Corinthians 4

Paul explains that we who are ambassadors of Christ have these treasures in "jars of clay," a truth he experienced very vividly in the weakness, sorrows, and depletion that he endured. I should have known that we would encounter the same. It didn't take long for that truth to set in. I learned that weariness of the spirit comes from preaching that is intense and passionate, from empathetically walking with others, from carrying a daily concern for the weak, and from the multiplicity of tasks that press in for attention. Such weariness will require times of refreshment and renewal, and the kind of rest that a Sabbath was designed for, and each pastor's methods of self-care must find the most appropriate way for this renewal to take place. Some congregations are more sensitive to that than others.

There is one more surprise we ought to think about. While the Bible talks about unity, love, and fellowship in the churches, it doesn't take long before we find the opposite is often what happens. Fellow Christians not only disagree with each other, but at times disagree in hostility, with rancor, and refuse to listen to or learn from each other. Proposals to a congregation may well meet with a very mixed reaction and those on both sides hold to their opinions vigorously; issues in the church will easily cause friends to separate to different sides of the issue; on a denominational level controversial issues will create meetings in which participants behave in ways that are less than Christian, even to the point of being schismatic. And the pastor is often caught in the middle of such situations. Both parties want the pastor to choose sides and it better be their side! Or at least they need the pastor's ear to convince him/her that their viewpoint is best for the church. I have been surprised at the frequency of such conflicts, at the vehemence of the disagreements, at what it does to the life of the church and the welfare of those who are involved. A pastor's personality makeup will likely have a great influence on how these times are handled and what good or damage come out of them. Some pastors can ably deal with conflict, some avoid it. Whichever, it will inevitably be a part of ministry. No surprise in that. But do be prepared for such surprises.

In His Service,
Your Colleague

Thinking About It—

> Try to recall the kinds of expectations you had when you first entered the Christian ministry. Were they realistic or not?

> Identify three to five surprises that your experiences in the ministry have involved for you. Share them with your colleagues (over your coffee cups) and compare notes.

15

Privileges Second to None

Dear Pastor,

I'm sure you have had certain special events that give you a glimpse of what is ahead in your ministry. Those events allow your ministry to take shape in your mind, but they also begin to form the feelings that you have about it all.

Such an event for me took place on September 20, 1962. The location was Lebanon, Iowa. I had been examined by the delegates of classis, the regional body of the church leaders, the day before and they approved me for ordination in the Ministry of the Word and Sacrament. So September 20 was the day of my ordination. This congregation was to be my "first church." Dr. Peter Eldersveld was the radio minister of the Christian Reformed Church, a widely recognized preacher. As my uncle, he agreed to travel to Lebanon for the event of my ordination and to bring the sermon. I remember much of what he said in that sermon and I've listened to it multiple times. But one comment stands out and will forever ring in my mind. He leaned forward over the pulpit, focusing on me as I sat in a front row. And then in his inimitable way he said, "And don't you ever forget that there are a lot of preachers out there who would give their right arm to be where you are as the pastor of a church like this one." I don't think he was making a statement about the supposed superiority of this particular congregation over others. He was addressing the supreme privilege of being a pastor in a Bible-believing congregation of faithful members. And it did not escape me! I kept that thought in my mind through all the years of my ministry—when I loved what I was doing and when it was more difficult than I expected, and when the congregation responded well to what I said and when they didn't. After living with that maxim for forty years, at the time of my retirement from the pastoral ministry, I had the very clear conviction in my heart that this has been the most profoundly rich way I could possibly have spent my life. I'm sure you can understand that it sometimes seems that few people have that kind of awareness.

And so it is not difficult for me to write a section in this material about the privileges of ministry. There are many. My hope and my intent is to help you renew your awareness of them. I'm praying that what I say will ring true with your heart.

First, I am privileged to see myself as *a product of the grace of God.* The ministry is not a let's-see-how-much-good-I-can-do profession; nor is it an I-can-lead-better-than-anyone-else trip. Those of us who must stand before the church every week and proclaim the truth are regularly convicted of our own unworthiness. We know we don't measure up to this, and when we say things that sound like that we are fooling ourselves as much as others. When we are faced with the biggest issues of life and death, of living wisely or crash-burning, we see our own weaknesses and failures far too clearly. So we preachers see ourselves as the product of the grace of God! Paul said it clearly and briefly, "It's by the grace of God that I am what I am" (1 Cor 15:10). I can be who I am, and say what I say, and stand where I stand, and serve how I serve, only because of the grace of God. To see that so clearly and unmistakably is a mighty big privilege. Somehow, for reasons known only to God, he reached down from heaven and touched me in my mother's womb. Even before that, he claimed me from before all time. And he called me to be one of his servants. Privileges don't come bigger than that! After all, it took his sovereign love, and the merciful work of his Son Jesus Christ on the cross. Such an awareness has anchored me in those times when ministry got much more difficult than I expected. When the load was heavy, and I became weary and discouraged, and wished I could just go somewhere else to a quiet vocation, the grace of God that had called me, also held me right there.

The ministry has also given me the privilege of serving as *the prophetic voice of God* from the pulpit. Sometimes we quickly label this profession as "being a preacher" and when I was young I'd simply tell people I was going to be a preacher. A generation or two ago, we were generally called preachers (with the assumption we did other things too); now the preferred title seems to be pastor (who also preaches.) But I've always considered myself as primarily a preacher. Needing to write and preach two different sermons each week supported that, of course, and my week's schedule was generally built around the need for sermon-writing time each morning. The majority of my seminary education was focused on understanding, interpreting, and communicating the Bible. Our theology insists that the Bible is holy, God's inspired and infallible word. It is truth and when I preach it I do not wonder if I am telling the truth. I have often watched and listened while those who think they have authority in our world change their theories and recommendations—e.g., at one time, researchers tell us coffee is bad for us and then the next group tells us it's good; one study says chocolate is unhealthy and another says it is healthy; certain vitamins are good for us and then another study reverses that. How can we know what is always good and what is always bad? Here I can stand with the Bible and be absolutely confident that what I bring is truth, unchanging truth. I have always marveled at what the prophet Isaiah said in ch. 55 of his prophecy:

> As the rain and the snow
> come down from heaven,
> and do not return to it
> without watering the earth
> and making it bud and flourish,
> so that it yields seed for the sower and bread for the eater,
> so is my word that goes out from my mouth:

It will not return to me empty,

but will accomplish what I desire

and achieve the purpose for which I sent it.

Those certainly are very profound words. A preacher finds great assurance in a promise like that, for every time we speak out the true word of God something will happen. God's purposes will be accomplished. I've stood in the pulpit over four thousand times with a sermon that speaks the Bible as truth and I've never had to wonder if someone will find out I brought them a lie, and I've never had to wonder if God would allow those efforts to be wasted. I've been in hospital rooms with patients who are critically ill and read promises for them that I know are sure. I've stood at gravesides with grieving families and read them passages about a resurrection with never a hint of doubt about their reliability. After all the fear and chaos from the terrorist attacks on September 11, 2001, I could enter the pulpit on Sunday morning with Psalm 46 and fearlessly proclaim that "God is our Refuge and our Strength" and know I was telling the absolute truth. There is no experience quite like knowing that God has given you his eternal and unchanging truth and called you to be a prophetic voice to proclaim it. I will never have to be ashamed that the words I proclaimed were not true and might be ineffective. To be sure, I regret that many of my sermons were less than they should be, but the truth they proclaimed was never less than golden.

In addition, those who are called to be ministers of the gospel, also have the distinct privilege of being *a priest* who stands between God and his children to bring them together, to help them talk to each other, and to help each other. Frankly, when I first entered the ministry, this one wasn't very large in my mind. I knew I'd be praying for people and for the congregation, but the significance of a priestly role never caught my attention. Yet, such a role became much more prominent in my mind as my ministry developed. I often became quite easily irritated when someone would hastily say, "Pastor, would you open with prayer?" It could happen at any church meeting and almost any social gathering. I often wondered if this happened because they assumed we always had a ready-made prayer in our pocket, or because we happened to be the person who found it easiest to find words in public settings. It may be either of those, but I gradually came to see that there was another element in it—the priestly role of the pastor, who therefore naturally was perceived as the "pray-er" in many gatherings.

Once I came to more accurately understand that role, many of my otherwise routine tasks took on greater significance. Each worship service usually includes a number of prayers for specific purposes, one of which is a major prayer, often called the Pastoral Prayer, Morning Prayer, or the Prayers of the People, etc. In the busy life of the pastor, with a wide variety of tasks for worship preparation, I must confess that it's far too easy to give little thought and minimal preparation for such prayers. That's probably OK if these are routine and rote events. But if these prayers are the occasion on which the priest steps into the presence of God to speak for his people and their needs, it becomes a much more significant task, one that calls for careful thought and preparation.

Not only the worship service, but other events as well, call for thoughtful priestly praying. I've stood by the bedside of many parishioners who need me to represent them and their needs to God. Physically, they need healing. Emotionally, they need security. Spiritually, they need a better ability to trust that God is at their side with his loving care. Their needs are many, their hearts are stunned, and some have even found they are unable to pray themselves. Whether they are able to admit that or not, I am needed as their priest. Perhaps that comes to the fore even more at the time of death. When death enters, hearts are sad and often are numbed. At such a time, the pastor in a priestly role is needed. It may be at a family gathering, or a funeral service, or at the grave side, but the grieving need their pastor to speak to God for them.

Once this priestly role becomes clear, the pastor realizes more and more what a privilege it is to stand between God and his people in their time of need.

I have said before that I discovered that as a pastor I had the privilege of *a front-row seat* for nearly every major event in the life of my parishioners. In some ways this involved observing it all as a spectator, but in another profound sense, I found myself involved as much more than an observer. I was a participant in the drama that was happening. Some of those events were exciting and delightful (such as baptisms, weddings, anniversaries, coming to faith, and such), but some were painful and heavy (such as accidents, tragedies, divorces, deaths, and such). And what was true for personal lives was also true for the congregation as a whole. When new ministries were begun, successes were achieved, and inspiring worship services took place, I was right there! Statistics can seem cold, but if I report that I have participated in 641 baptisms, 510 professions and affirmations of faith, 282 marriages, and 180 funerals, you can easily imagine the hundreds of people who were also involved as participants in these events which would shape their lives and spiritual commitments long through the future. Big events like these were not something I observed from a distance, but something for which I had a front row seat.

One more surprise needs to be mentioned. It involves the *positive formation of our children and grandchildren* when we serve in the ministry. My wife and I had great concern about this when we entered the ministry. Stories abound about clergy families who have reacted very positively to a life in the manse; and many other stories abound that are sad indeed. In one family the children learn to share the faith of their parents and develop a firm loyalty to the church. In another the opposite happens. We've seen both, and because we've seen both we carried anxiety about the matter into the ministry with us. I am pleased to say that our story is a positive one. Our three sons all are deeply committed to the Christian faith, are rooted in Jesus Christ, and have entered lives of Christian service of one sort or another. We now are seeing much the same in our grandchildren. We give thanks to God for this, but do so very aware of colleagues whose experiences are quite different and whose families are the source of disappointment instead of encouragement.

I wish it were possible to identify what it is that assures a positive response to ministry on the part of children and grand-children. To do so would be to claim I understand the process, but indeed I do not. When families respond well with wholesome commitments, we give thanks to God for his blessing. And when they do not respond well, it is wise perhaps to withhold explanations and judgments. Yet, having said that, it is important for all those in ministry to faithfully pay attention to the emotional and spiritual needs of their children and never to allow the demands of the ministry to overshadow the work of Christian parenting.

Surely, there are other privileges that could be cited. Each of us will have a list of the most special experiences of the ministry. When we put them all together, they will be many. It is, indeed, a very privileged calling.

In His Service,
Your Colleague

Thinking About It—

> Make a list of the most special experiences of your ministry?

> Identify to yourself why these experiences were such a privilege and share them with others.

16

The Cost of Ministry

DEAR PASTOR,

I have read, and preached on, that passage in Luke 14:25ff. in which Jesus teaches his disciples about the cost of being his disciple. You know the story—if someone wants to build a tower, he has to sit down and calculate the cost first because if he does not and doesn't have the resources to finish, he will look silly. And he tells of a king who goes out to war against another king but must count the cost first, for if he doesn't and does not have the resources to win, he'll have to give up. When we've preached on that, we've probably always associated it with the life of following Christ. But have you thought of the fact that it may be speaking of the Christian ministry? I'm a bit ambivalent about that. I tend to think of the Christian ministry as rich, with good rewards. I hesitate to think in terms of the cost of ministry.

But there are costs and it doesn't take long for them to become apparent. Perhaps you are experiencing some of them already. And perhaps some of those costs have discouraged you, or even tempted you to question your calling.

One subtle cause of pain comes from the fact that the true followers of Jesus Christ are a minority in world society. We are warned about this by Jesus and the Scriptures. The Bible makes it very clear that those who follow the narrow way of Christ will be few compared to those who do not. These words are easily understood by Christians and their leaders who live in lands where the percentage of confessing Christians is 1 or 2 percent. Christian leaders always live and serve with the awareness that they are a minority and such a position will involve certain costs.

However, in Western society, where we tend to hold on to the myth that our heritage is "Christian" (of sorts) and that our society today is a basically Christian (of sorts) society, we set ourselves up for some big disappointments. As long as we remain closely connected in our small and isolated communities, surrounding ourselves only with those who think and act like we do, we feel safe and we can convince ourselves that society feels the same. But when the church moves into the world in Christian mission and action, and when our lives intersect with others on the foundational issues of our day, we discover such is not the case. Our security is easily shattered when we discover that our values and our message is countercultural. Our early assurance that all are like us soon becomes a painful realization that most are not like us. Individual Christians experience this pain, but a pastor who aims to lead his/her church to a greater engagement with the issues, forces, and evils of the day experiences this pain in an even greater measure.

Vicarious pain in the normal course of pastoral work also brings pain. I hesitate to call vicarious pain one of the costs, but it is. Pastors who love their parishioners will inevitably take on a portion of the pain their people are experiencing. When a young father of thirty-seven dies of cancer, an elder has a heart attack, a marriage is crumbling, a young girl is a victim of sexual abuse, a young child is stricken with a major disease, or the congregation fractures—and so many other similar events occur—the pastor will take on a measure of the pain from each of these lives. You can't be a good pastor and not take on their pain. The most severe pain, of course, comes when shipwreck occurs in the faith-life of parishioners and/or their children. People who appeared to be faithful in their commitments, whose words made a clear affirmation of faith, now for some reason are abandoning their faith-life and openly rejecting the gospel and the call to follow Christ. It has often been said that parents feel no greater pain than when their children abandon their faith. The same is true for a faithful pastor who loves the sheep.

After some time, the "pain meter" goes up rather high. To be a pastor is to take on the pain of other folks. It's a Christlike thing. We all need to develop coping methods so that the pain doesn't become overwhelming for that will inhibit our ability to do ministry well. At the same time a pastor who does not feel the pain of others is not loving them as Christ intended.

Personal conflict is another cause of pain. I knew this was a possibility in the ministry because I observed that my father, who frequently served as an elder, was involved in church conflict from time to time. So I knew such things existed. But to personally experience it was something quite different, especially when it became clear that in times of conflict people can become very intense in their feelings and reactions. And when they do, they are able to say things and do things that can be very disturbing. Two separate events during the first year of my ministry brought this awareness home with great surprise. One day a parishioner appeared at the door of my home, quite irate about a position I had taken. This normally pleasant man, whom I had come to know as a very supportive parishioner said things about our decision, about me, and about our church council for which I was quite unprepared. Sometime later I was making a home visit to another family only to learn they had a long list of complaints about the church, the council, and about me. I had only been their pastor a year and hardly felt I could have done so much wrong in that short a time. Their anger was not to be calmed. Within the first year of ministry, I learned quite abruptly that one of the costs of ministry is to become the subject of the conflict and anger that exists in the church today.

Those two events in my first year of ministry should have prepared me for repeated occurrences of the same. I have been repeatedly surprised at how frequently conflict can arise in the church and how vehement it can become. Perhaps I can even label this as my most severe disappointment with the church, and my biggest surprise. All four congregations had their times of conflict, more or less. And when I was put in a role of leadership on the broader denominational level I experienced it there even more. During the '80s and '90s our denomination went through prolonged debates and struggles over some explosive issues. I happened to be an officer of its broadest body during that time and the angry conflict I experienced disillusioned me significantly. I know that I am a person who does not do well with conflict, my personality tests show I tend to be a peacemaker, and I thought I could expect the church to be marked by the kind of fellowship and communion that involved understanding, love, forbearance, and compatible efforts to work together. Instead, what I saw and experienced replaced joy with pain.

It should not escape us that the New Testament speaks about the suffering that may and will come to obedient servants of Christ. As Christ suffered for us and for this world, so we can expect to experience the same. Peter speaks to the scattered church about the "painful trials" they are experiencing, and then speaks of that as "participating in the sufferings of Christ" (1 Pet 4:13). And Paul speaks to the Colossian Christians about the suffering he has experienced for their sake, and calls it an act of filling up "in my flesh what is still lacking in regards to Christ's afflictions, for the sake of his body, which is the church" (Col 1:24). So the servant of Christ in the ministry of Christ can expect to experience that the cost of ministry will involve some of the sufferings of Christ. Yes, the Christian Church can be a messy place and those who serve often pay a price for being there.

And at times pastors may be stricken with the pain of disillusionment. Ministry efforts seems to go nowhere. The response of parishioners is disappointing. Faithfully written sermons seem not to connect. Encouraging, praying, even prodding, seem ineffective in getting the saints to take on new challenges and illustrate greater obedience. We can handle these disappointments for a time, but finally we begin to doubt ourselves, questions our efforts, and then question our fitness for ministry. This becomes a unique searing sort of pain that can destroy our motivation for ministry if it continues.

Still other dimensions of pain in the ministry had to do with my family life and its impact there. My family means everything to me and I wanted our life of service to be healthy for them and hopefully to set a model before them that would motivate them for kingdom service. However, I had some fears and concerns because I had learned from some other families that life in the parsonage had not been so healthy for them. My mother was raised in a parsonage, and of seven children, the majority of her siblings were not well-grounded spiritually. Though they achieved excellent academic degrees and entered professional lives, only a few of them had any love and respect for the life of the church. I thought of that often and wanted to avoid that in our family.

I could see rather quickly that it was easy for folks to have a different set of expectations for my family simply because they lived in the parsonage and I was concerned about how that would impact them. We were careful never to set boundaries or rules for them on the basis of "because you are the preacher's son." Our only ground was "because you are a Christian." Hopefully that took away some of the temptation to resist. But I soon found there were other obstacles that we would have to deal with. It is often said that the ministry is a 24/7 vocation, and while there were only a few times when I was called out during the night, there were many times when my obligation conflicted with family plans. I normally had meetings or obligations most weekday evenings and a schedule like that prevented me from being the parent who would end the day with them and tuck them into bed. I tried to compensate by keeping a free dinner hour and use it as time for them. Only occasionally did family vacation times get interrupted by my work. So we managed to work through it all, and I'm grateful to say that all three sons now in their adult life carry very positive memories of life in the parsonage and all three have entered a variety of forms of kingdom service.

I hesitate to raise the issue of finances and salaries, but I know it is part of the overall picture. I have always felt that we have been treated very fairly by the churches, perhaps better than some others. Yet, it certainly was true that there were years when our finances barely covered the needs we had. At such times, I found myself dreaming about the other professions I could have entered with the same amount of academic degrees I had, and the increased amount of remuneration we might receive. We tried to use such times as a teaching time with the children. As a family we often loved to take a ride out to the beach for a family picnic supper and spend time watching the pleasure boats travel in and out of the channel. Our boys were quite enthused about boats and would watch them with longing. They knew my favorite response to them was, "See that boat . . . there goes your Christian education . . . all it would take is a couple of years." I was confident that they loved school and knew well the value of a Christian education that the point of my comment would stick. It did.

To be sure there are privileges, and joys, and pleasant surprises in the gospel ministry. But there also is a cost. It is wise to be up front and count the cost ahead of time to be sure we have the commitment required.

In His Service,
Your Colleague

Thinking About It—

> Identify some of the costs and the pain that the Christian ministry has involved for you? If you are free to do so, share these with your colleagues over your coffee cups.

> In what way could some of your painful experiences in the ministry be said to participate in the sufferings of Christ or fill up the afflictions of Christ for the church?

17

Finding Balance

DEAR PASTOR,

Shortly into your ministry you have likely found there is another issue that you need to deal with. If you do not come to realize this one, your spouse will likely remind you, or your children might. But no one else will. As a matter of fact, sometimes the church seems determined to create imbalance in our lives instead of balance.

But you will certainly face it. How many hours should I work each week? How many evenings may I be gone from my family? How many dinner times may I miss? How often may I take phone calls during dinner time? How long can we go without a vacation? How many extra commitments may I take? And your wife will likely feel the same pressure. How many groups should I attend? What type of leadership do they expect of me? Must I go along on calls to shut-ins? Do they understand that I have young children at home? And so it goes.

It can be a big problem. And a dangerous risk goes along with it.

Just think with me about some of the consequences of failing to find a proper balance in your ministry. One of the casualties will likely be you, because you will soon experience what is called "burnout." God never intended that we work at full speed all week without breaks to relax, renew ourselves, and catch our breath. I'm reminded of the cartoon I saw one day of a haggard pastor in the emergency room who says to the doctor, "But, doctor, I didn't come to be told not to burn the candle at both ends. I came for more candles!" Burnout can be very real for those who push hard without adequate breaks for renewal. And along with that comes the risk of beginning to resent the church and/or the ministry because we feel that unreasonable demands have been placed on us. Many a weary minister has mumbled through harried days, "This isn't really what I signed up for."

It's also a perfect way for a spouse to feel like a widow. Sure, he or she agreed to join you in ministry, but they perceived that it would be a mutually rewarding life of service. They didn't sign up to be deserted, to spend long hours home alone, or to put the kids to bed alone every night. It doesn't take long before a spouse becomes disillusioned.

And your children are sure to feel it too. It's not hard to find kids in the church today who feel deserted by their overworking pastor-father or mother. I have seen it. First they resent their parent who is gone so much, then it turns into a resentment of the ministry, and then resentment of the church, and even of God. How much better is the example of those who have come to respect and admire a pastor-parent who has served with a healthy balance and the children also choose to follow in their parents footsteps and enter the ministry.

We've struggled with these issues in our home too. We have three sons and we came to realize that they were watching us closely and their attitude toward the church and the ministry would be shaped by what they saw in us. And I saw my wife struggle with it too. When my ministry began I was quite enthralled with the way in which people seemed to need me . . . for all kind of needs. I was quite enthused about being needed so much and I spent more and more time away from my family. But then she felt very alone. And she faced her owns struggles with how much she should be serving and what her role should be. As a young mother should she be a part of every group? And began to wonder about the message being given to our sons.

Then one day at a casual gathering of pastors and their spouses, my wife had a conversation with another pastor's wife. She was much older and her husband had retired from the ministry. They struck up a conversation together and the older friend reflected on all the pastor's wives who tell about all the wonderful things they are involved in, but she also reflected on how she's seen quite a number of them who had to be treated and counseled for depression, disillusionment, resentment, and other emotional problems. Then she went on to say to my wife what turned out to be golden lifelong advice. "I believe," she said, "that God has called me to be first of all a wife to my husband; secondly, a mother to my children; and thirdly, a member of the church."

I know that the Christian ministry is not the only profession in which the temptation to imbalance is so strong. Many leaders in almost every profession face the same thing. But in the ministry our witness and our effectiveness is tied to our success in achieving balance between pastoral responsibilities, a healthy marriage, effective parenting, and other friendships.

With those considerations in mind, I suggest these guidelines:

- It is no sin to work hard (see ch. 5). An effective ministry certainly takes intentional effort and a willingness to be available for the needs of members of the congregation and the community.

- The availability of the pastor in times of emergency is highly important. Such times are often the key opportunities for ministry and the pastor's convenience and personal schedule must be secondary to the needs of the moment.

- Your marriage needs adequate nurture time. It may be a quiet evening at home or away, or a date night, or adequate time to talk together and share thoughts and feelings without interruption.

- A healthy marriage needs enough private and casual time to assure one's spouse that she is still precious to you regardless of how long you have been married.

- As soon as church activities begin to interfere with important family activities, somebody needs to learn to discern which church activities are essential and which are optional.

- Pastors do have the right to say "no" on occasion to church activities for the sake of their home and family life.

- Growing children need some uninterrupted time with their parent. Even the church should not expect them to give that up.

- It is highly advisable that parents and children find hobbies which they can share together. Such activities will give them relaxation and time together.

- Only emergencies should have the right to interrupt meal times. The telephone does not need to always be answered.

Achieving balance in the ministry is a large responsibility with a hidden danger. Marriage, ministry, family, friendships, and relaxation all call for a portion of our time and attention but often call for more than they should be allowed. Wise is the pastor who through careful analysis, prayer, and conversation finds a healthy balance that does justice to each of these. Such a ministry will be more effective, and the same will be said for the other areas of life.

In His Service,
Your Colleague

Thinking About It—

> Honestly now, how do you feel about the balance you have achieved in your ministry? How does your spouse feel about it? How about your family? Would they agree?

> Consider the nine guidelines given above. Which of those do you believe needs more attention in your life and ministry?

18

Finding a Sabbath for Pastors

DEAR PASTOR,

Another dilemma crept up on me by surprise. What about a Sabbath? Can pastors have a Sabbath? I never thought about the struggle I would face around this issue.

I grew up in a home and a church in which the Sabbath was a big deal. We knew about the fourth commandment and our practice of it received high priority. Our family was pretty traditional in this regard. We attended church twice each Sunday (no excuses!). Our family schedule on Sunday was always built around those two worship services, a family dinner and family time together the rest of the day. At times it seemed rather legalistic, but we knew it all was marked by deep convictions.

And now I was entering the Christian ministry and would be pastoring a church which held two worship services every Sunday. Because of my leadership role in those worship services, I would be busy working on Sunday every week. I never gave much thought to all that. But suddenly it became clear to me that in addition to preparing for leadership and preaching for both services, and often another meeting or class in addition, my Sunday became a very busy day. During the last fifteen years of my ministry when our congregation held two worship services each morning, in addition to the evening service, the issue grew even more complex.

I conveniently ignored the issue for the first number of years in the ministry. I worked on Sunday, usually took a little time off on Monday (I was weary!) and then worked right through the rest of the week. That pattern continued for a number of years while fatigue accumulated. One day, while sharing my concerns over my fatigue with a close friend, he jolted me by kindly and firmly asking, "Do you think the fourth commandment does not apply to pastors?" I had no good answer, except to mumble something about the fact that Sunday is for going to worship and I'm surely doing that every week. But I knew it was an unsatisfactory answer and I needed to think more honestly about the subject. So I explored the Scriptures, and our tradition, and what others had said on the matter. I read widely to learn how others had dealt with the dilemma. Two books I found most helpful were *A Royal "Waste" of Time*, by Marva J. Dawn, and *Receiving the Day*, by Dorothy C. Bass.

I gradually clarified for myself that God's intent in establishing Sabbath practices among his people really has about six different, but closely related, dimensions to it.

- The Sabbath provides a time for the worship of God and fellowship with the gathered people of God. The Old Testament people gathered in the temple for their worship times; the Jews gathered in synagogues; and throughout history God's people have gathered for worship on the first day of the week to mark the resurrection of Christ from the dead.

- The Sabbath is a time for physical rest so that our physical bodies can be refreshed from the fatigue of a week of work. Already in the opening chapters of the Bible, God illustrates by his own behavior that he has built into creation the rhythm of six to one—six days of work and one day of rest. He built that language into the moral law through the wording of the fourth commandment and confirmed it by his own behavior.

- The Sabbath is also a time for spiritual refreshment, a time to reflect, to recenter ourselves in life under the care and sovereignty of God. The very nature of work in this fallen world is such that it serves to constantly distract us, to distort our values, to move God off the throne, and replace him with all our personal idols. And all this happens so subtly that we are not even aware of it. So those who aim to live faithfully as God's children in this world are in need of a time of correction by renewing our perspective of life as lived obediently before the face of God.

- The Sabbath also provides a time for mental renewal. Perhaps in previous generations when work consisted of primarily manual labor the urgency was not so great for mental fatigue and distortion was not quite as prominent. But the scene of work and labor has changed so much today that many experience mental fatigue even more than physical fatigue. Consequently, we need not only to rest our bodies from the rigors of our labor but we also need to provide refreshment for our minds or they will increasingly wear down, become distorted, and thinking will become twisted.

- The Sabbath provides a time for service to others, a time when an unselfish concern for the poor becomes prominent. During the week schedules can become full, energies are drained, and we easily become preoccupied with our own needs. How necessary for God's people in the world to remember that they are a delivered people, and this special day can be a time for us to step outside of our self-centered concerns and open our hands and our hearts to others who are in need, to visit those who are otherwise forgotten and extend hospitality to those who might be lonely.

- And the Sabbath provides a time for us to focus more personally on healthy relationships. We join others within the body of Christ so our worship becomes corporate; we are concerned about needy humans among us so our day involves service; but we also center on that most important location of the deepest relationships in our family and we spend quality time together with those who are closest to us yet are frequently pushed aside in the busy schedules of our work-week. So family time becomes a high value on the Sabbath.

Once I had discovered what I believe God had in mind with the Sabbath, it was time to talk to myself. Maybe you are feeling the same thing. Several givens were very obvious to me—God was serious when he gave us a Sabbath, and, yes, the fourth command-ment also applies to preachers. My great fatigue was probably an indicator that something was awry, and the fact that Sunday was a busy day of "work" for me meant that the old rules, traditions and patterns for the Sabbath probably wouldn't work in my life. So what should I do? How could I go about finding a satisfactory solution?

I entered a period of experimentation. Little by little, I nar-rowed down my concerns, tried a variety of patterns that might help, and gradually arrived at a pattern that led me to believe I was doing justice to my work schedule, and also gave me the benefits God intended by Sabbath-living.

The pattern I developed did not change my life on Sunday at all. Sunday continued to be a busy day, rising early, making prepa-rations, leading in worship, only to catch a quick rest and have the pattern start over for the evening worship service. The day was full and demanding, and made me weary, yet filled with a deep sense of privilege for the role God had given me. I did, however, exert more care in managing what other activities entered my schedule that might compete with a busy Sunday. Saturday night activities were excluded if at all possible, and all other meetings were excluded from Sunday in so far as they could be. That way I was free to focus all my energies on worship and leading worship. I did continue, however, to face the constant challenge to find a way in which I could personally worship while leading worship. Sometimes that went better than at other times, but generally I found it took intentional efforts, careful preparation, and regular renewed efforts at it. If I were insufficiently prepared, I found it harder to worship personally. And if I did not deliberately remind myself before a service to "be sure to worship yourself," I slipped in my efforts to do so.

The pattern for the rest of the week took shape, through experimentation, in such a way that the other purposes of a Sabbath were fulfilled. By Sunday night and Monday morning I was very fatigued, physically and mentally, though I was refreshed spiritually. I dedicated most of Monday, therefore, as a day free from mental work and only limited physical work. The pace was slow, my family was more in focus, personal tasks received my attention, my favorite hobbies of yard work, reading, and model railroading often received my efforts. Monday evening found me ready to return to my study for private efforts at correspondence, record-keeping, filing, and such non-demanding efforts. By the time Tuesday morning arrived I was ready to return to my normal schedule for work again. Monday has, therefore, provided half of my Sabbath rest. The remainder of the Sabbath rest came on Friday evening, almost always free for family time, and on Saturday afternoon and evening. I made a concerted effort to have all sermon and worship preparation completed by noon on Saturday. At that time, I set it all aside and freed my mind and heart for personal time. Saturday afternoon was much the same as Monday—leisure, hobbies, and personal tasks. Saturday evening was the same, until the close of the evening when I spent some time reviewing the worship service and my sermon for the follow morning one more time.

To sum it up, the spiritual portion of the Sabbath continued to be satisfied on Sunday in worship and I remained committed to both morning and evening worship, not as a legal requirement, but as the best way to assure myself of a healthy Sabbath. The other portions of the Sabbath were satisfied by the first half of Monday and the second half of Saturday. Such times were interrupted only when necessary, by responsibilities such as hospital calls, a wedding, or a funeral.

Each pastor must find his or her own personal way to accomplish the Sabbath role in a ministry life. It will be very easy to ignore it, forsake it, and pay a price later on. You may adopt a pattern quite different from what I have explained here. Which pattern is followed may vary, but the six dimensions of the Sabbath spelled out above will form the most beneficial Sabbath pattern.

I encourage you to honestly evaluate your own current practices, consider the six dimensions spelled out, and experiment with your schedule, taking into consideration your schedule, your personality, your family and spouse needs, until you arrive at a pattern that will fit best.

In His Service,
Your Colleague

Thinking About It—

> What is your Sabbath-pattern?
>
> What are the benefits in your present Sabbath pattern?

19

Serving in Suburbia

DEAR PASTOR,

I have a sense that there is one more question that we ought to face together. Three of my four pastorates were considered to be suburban parishes, that is, they were on the outskirts of a larger city. Trinity Church in Jenison was in a suburb of Grand Rapids, Michigan. Bethel Church in Lansing was a suburb of Chicago, Illinois. Hillcrest Church in Hudsonville was a suburb of Grand Rapids, Michigan. Only my first pastorate, in Lebanon, Iowa, was not suburban but rather rural.

Suburban churches have a unique character and ministry and such locations bring a special kind of challenge. I found God clearly leading me to this type of ministry, but I also found that suburban ministries are often misunderstood and maligned. They suffer from stereotypes in the minds of many and therefore I believe an explanation might help you. You could be finding yourself in the midst of a struggle with what kind of ministry you would find most satisfying, so let me offer you some reflections through my rearview mirror. The kind of misunderstanding I'm referring to came subtly in the form of comments from other colleagues when they would say, "Yes, but you serve in a suburban parish," as though that makes my experience different from everyone else and they can readily discount my reflections. In the minds of many,

certain types of ministry have more glamor and are more front-
line, like church planting, a world mission field, or some multicul-
tural setting. Some of my colleagues left me with the impression
that suburban pastorates are "comfort parishes," that is, they are
pleasant to serve, prosperous, with plenty of resources, successful in what they do but somewhat limited in vision. While they
may be pleasant, they fail to deal with the big issues of injustice,
poverty, brokenness, unbelief, cross-cultural ministries, and other
challenges that churches face. While I readily agree that suburban
pastorates have their weaknesses and challenges, I could not disagree more with the stereotype some have. So let's examine the
subject together.

When I was in seminary, and at the time I entered the ministry in 1962, our choices were rather limited. We could become a
preacher and serve a pastorate, generally rural, in a small town or
suburbia. We could become a missionary and plant churches here
at home or somewhere else in the world. We could become a chaplain and enter military service or develop a counseling ministry.
Or there might be a few among us who would choose to continue
their education and become a professor or a teacher. The options
were quite clearly distinguished and the choice was ours to make.

I found myself very challenged by and attracted to the suburban pastorate and I became more and more confirmed in that. After I had spent a few years in my first rural pastorate, a number of
pastoral calls came my way and confronted me with hard choices.
Should I go to the mission field, or become a chaplain, or teach, or
remain in an established pastorate? Each time that I had to make a
decision on a pastoral call, the issues gradually became clearer to
me. How I perceived of my gifts, how I sensed God's call to me, the
passion he had laid on my heart, and the personality I was given all
seemed to lead me in the same direction. At the same time, some
timely conversations with several senior colleagues shed more
light on the issue for me. One very experienced pastor warned me
to be very cautious about the selection of my second place to serve.
"Your second charge will be the one that most likely will form you
the most," he said. I found it was wise advice, and again God was

leading me through the informal comments of colleagues. As a result, thirty-six of my forty years in the pastorate were located in suburban parishes!

I found they were not "comfort parishes." Though they were rewarding, they were not always pleasant; though they were usually very resourceful, they proved also to be frustrating; and though they seemed limited in vision, at other times the opposite was true; and though they may give the appearance of security, a suburban pastor carries a much heavier load than most realize.

So let me say a few words in explanation of what a suburban pastorate involves. I hope these words will dispel some of the myths that persist, will increase your respect for those who serve in such pastorates, and will open your eyes to the unique opportunities that suburbia provides.

Suburban churches, though they appear to be comfortable and pleasant, are marked by all the same church sins that appear anywhere else. They are indeed tempted to become very complacent and traditional. They certainly are prone to insidiously become communities that are highly competitive with the other churches in town whether they are of the same family or not. Even the pastors of such churches are subtly prone to such competitiveness. It is true that these churches easily become communities that are insular, quite detached from the issues of justice, violence, and prejudice. They can become so introverted that a vision of the needs of the world languishes among them. At the same time, each of its members continues to experience the same spiritual struggles that others have. The challenge is to lead them past that.

Two conversations show the reality of pastoral work in such congregations. Two of my elders were having a conversation one evening and I was privileged to listen in. Both were in their sixties and they began admitting to each other that "by this stage in life I surely thought I'd have some of my sinful struggles resolved, but it just doesn't go that way so easily." I was surprised. After a youth service in which the youth of the church were highlighted in our worship and the struggles of youth were addressed, a senior widow stopped me after church to say, "That was nice, but don't ever forget that us old folks have a pretty tough time of it too." And perhaps that's why one of the heaviest burdens of suburbia easily tends to be the temptation to look all put together on the outside when we're all falling part on the inside. Appearance means so much in suburbia that we find it difficult to be honest before God . . . and one another. In addition, in suburbia the temptation to consider ourselves to be self-sufficient is powerful. Suburban folks have so much that middle-class America offers, and have heard so many messages about self-confidence that much of what we say and do with the message of the gospel seems contradictory. Indeed, the gospel of suburbia often is that of self-sufficiency. Consequently, ministry in a suburban pastorate will not be easy. A pastor who takes her calling seriously will see spiritual struggles everywhere, though often dressed up attractively. The message of grace is foreign to the ears that normally hear of self-help. Christian humility sounds strange to those who pride themselves on personal accomplishments. The need for repentance and humility sound foreign to suburban folks. And so the pressures and frustration of the ministry in suburbia continue to grow until the workload of the pastor leads to fatigue, discouragement and burnout. The demands of such work can cause the pastor to be vulnerable to depression.

And yet, even with those dangers, I found the suburban pastorate such a richly satisfying place to serve. I served there not only because God called me there but because I loved it and found it rewarding. As a matter of fact, I spent twenty-four years in my fourth pastorate. So why did I find it so satisfying? And why do I wish the stereotype of suburban pastorates could be corrected?

Suburbia is where so many churches and Christians are found. I lack statistics, but I believe that the majority of the members of our denomination will be found in suburban or small-town congregations. All these people are members of the body of Christ, valuable to him, and in need of nurture and care. All these have their personal struggles and need for encouragement, support, and growth. All these possess gifts and abilities that are to be harnessed for the work of God's kingdom in the world. And all these are in need of hearing and knowing the gospel of a new life in Jesus Christ and being "built up until we all reach unity in the faith and in the knowledge of the Son of God and become mature" (Eph 4:12–13).

Suburbia is marked by a concentration of families. Some are two-parent, some are single-parent, and some are more functional than others. But families are the building blocks of society as a whole. In his economy, God places a high value on families. He created the world with a family and has made his covenant with families. So all the families, highly concentrated in suburbia, are important to the church and the pastor. Therefore the suburban parish will likely have a large number of children and youth to whom they are able to minister. The ministry to families, directly and indirectly, aims to serve their spiritual health, teach them to function well together, establish God-centered values, and prepare them to make a contribution to society as a whole.

Suburbia is not immune from spiritual warfare. Those who live there may feel pressure to appear all put together but beneath the surface lurks all the moral and ethical crises that any other segment of society faces. If they are ever to fulfill their purposes in society on any level they will need intense Christlike care that will help destroy their facade, identity their hypocrisy and brokenness, lead them to desire healing and recovery, and bring them to an experience of saving grace in Jesus Christ.

Suburbia includes a high percentage of small business personnel. Small businesses of all sorts are the engine of our society. If they are healthy and ethical small businesses, the society will be served well. If they are not, society will suffer. Therefore the men and women who form and manage these small business are inordinately influential people in our society. Life for society as a whole, and for individual lives and families, will be fair and just only to the extent that the business of our communities are healthy and fair. The suburban pastorate, therefore, has the golden opportunity to minister to the men and women who establish, maintain, and operate these businesses, some of which will be located in the suburbs and others in the cities.

Suburbia also is able to provide the resources needed for the worldwide mission of the church. A given suburban church may not have a pressing outreach opportunity in its own neighborhood, yet it has the persons and finances that can support other mission efforts, provide the personnel that mission organizations need, and the funds to make it possible. When a suburban church is challenged to be generous in its stewardship, many mission efforts at a distance receive life; and when the youth of a suburban church are challenged in forming their life view, the suburban church and the mission field of a distant land join hands. The worldwide mission efforts of the church need suburban parishes.

Suburbia participates in a growing and scattering pattern which extends its influence far beyond itself. As a community with families, where education is valued, children and youth are educated, many go off to college for advanced training, and as they find their vocations in many places around the world, the influence of their home (suburban) church has had a significant role in shaping them and sending them out. A given suburban pastorate can count its youth-now-grown among those who have scattered around the nations and the globe to serve and lead. At holiday time, a suburban pastorate will see many of the "scattered ones" arriving home for the holidays thereby reminding all of how far the influence of this community has spread.

Suburbia, therefore, becomes a highly influential place when a world-and-life-view ministry takes place there. The potential is far-reaching. It is in such a setting that the message of Paul in Ephesians 4:11–12 took on such significance. I began to think of my ministry as an "equipping" ministry. God had plans for all these people, he had distributed gifts to them to use in his service, and he was busy in the process of grooming them to be the kind of persons he could use, and my role was to equip them to best be able to fulfill the roles God had designed for them. A world-and-life view taught me never to think too narrowly of the way in which God might use them, but to see the broad and expansive view God had. It was not for me to select the ways in which they might serve but to build them up spiritually (i.e., in sanctification) so that wherever they serve they will be doing it as mature Christians.

So, if God calls you to some other location and form of ministry, follow him with all your heart. He will gift you, bless you, and use you. But if he should be calling you to ministry in one of the large number of suburban pastorates, do not allow any misconceptions or inaccurate stereotypes to dissuade you. It will not be without its challenges and its demands, but you will find it a location for ministry filled with potential.

In His Service,
Your Colleague

Thinking About It—

> To where do you feel called?

> What has led you to that conviction?

20

The Pastor and the Community

DEAR PASTOR,

When we receive and accept a Letter of Call from a congrega-tion, a form of bonding begins immediately. We easily call it "our congregation" and as pastor and congregation, we sense that we belong to each other. Often one of our expressed goals in pastoral work is to reinforce such bonds with each other so our sense of community is deepened.

But what about the broader community in which your pas-torate is located? Is there such a thing as a call to serve that broader community too? Do pastors belong just to their congregation, or to their congregation and the community in which it is located?

Here's another question which has confronted pastors in re-cent years with an urgency that did not appear before. In times past, a congregation often lived with a certain degree of isolation from the community around it, especially if the issue of ethnic identity was present. Often separation rather than bonding was the theme of many pastorates.

Not so today. Three issues have brought this question to the forefront today. The first is the changing expectations for the con-gregation. In the past a congregation might have been very satis-fied with retaining its current membership and ministering well to those who are already members with little concern for drawing neighbors in. Generally, such is not the case today for the church is learning that it is in the world to reach others, to minister to those who are not members, and hopefully to draw them into the church. Consequently, the work of the pastor and the success of programs is based on a willingness to reach neighbors and extend the influence of the church. One spin-off of this changed viewpoint is a different set of expectations for the pastor. He/she is expected to have a concern of the heart for both the congregation and the community.

At the same time, a second consideration has entered and it involves the changing nature of many communities. Whereas a generation ago a given community might have been marked by sameness in its makeup, economically and ethnically, gradually many neighborhoods are changing. Twenty years ago most folks were acquainted with each other, now many are strangers. Before this shift the standard of living might have been very consistent, now some are in severe need while others are not. As a result the community has families and households who need help and assistance, yet have few friends to provide this help. Earlier the majority may even have been related to a church, now church members are a minority. Consequently the risk is high of some with special needs being overlooked.

And at the same time, a third transition is taking place. The pastor is viewed as someone who in some sense belongs to the entire community and not merely to a single congregation. When this shift happens, folks within the community who have no church relationship will be more ready to call on the pastor for some help, or at least expect the pastor to show some caring interest in them. Whereas a generation ago the community might have looked at the pastor and assumed "that's their pastor" (meaning a certain congregation, or a certain neighbor from that church) now they are much more likely to some degree to consider the pastor as a fixed part of the community as a whole, i,e, the pastor of all of us.

All three of these shifts have brought a new day for the local congregation, but have also faced pastors with a new set of circumstances and expectations. When we consider a pastoral call, do we view this as a call to serve a particular congregation, or a broader community? As we consider this pastoral call do we study the congregation and its needs, or do we broaden that out to examine the needs of the community too? When we move to a new pastorate, do we focus all our efforts to get acquainted with the congregation and its needs, or must we also analyze the community and attempt to discern its needs also? In other words, how narrow or how broad is the view we have of our mandate?

Consequently, the generation of pastors who enter the ministry today normally have a much broader focus than those who entered a generation or two ago. And at the same time, we are seeing greater diversity and variation in the way pastors respond to this issue. Some will still limit their focus narrowly on their congregation, and others will look much more like a community activist. My patterns in the four congregations I have served were very different patterns, shaped by the community I was in, and my understanding of my role. As I review them, I would likely take a much broader role today than I did at the time. I see and sense new pastors today taking this shift in expectations very seriously. I am encouraged for I consider this to be healthy for the mission of the church.

So here is a pressing new question that all pastors must address as they evaluate their ministries—do I primarily serve the congregation, or the community too? Does the congregation deserve all my time, or do I spend some on the community too? How big is the circle of people whom I am called to love? And how far does my availability extend?

As always, there are no fixed and set patterns for pastors to implement. Denominational officials will not be able to set guidelines. And even an individual pastor will likely find her role shifting from one pastorate to another. There are, however, several factors that will likely have a shaping influence on this matter.

- The personality of the pastor will be key. Some personalities are more engaged, thrive on interaction with others, are passionately moved by the needs of others, and highly motivated to help others and serve community causes.

- The personality of the congregation will also influence the pattern that is developed. Is the congregation multigenerational, are its younger generations engaged with the community members, do the members of the congregation live in the community around the church or are they commuters, are congregational members active in the issues of the neighborhood, and are they local business people?

- And the personality of the community must also be considered. To what degree are the members churched? How stable is the community? Is it transitional? How needy is it and which needs are most pressing? What is its general attitude toward the church and religion?

Each pastor will need to craft his or her own style of ministry in the community, but surely it will need to include a clear understanding of the needs of the community and which of those needs require attention first. It will need an understanding of the demographics of the community, family structures, youth, and opportunities the church can step into. But more personally, the pastor will want to assess where the best openings are to be found for meaningful ministry. How can relationships be built? How can the pastor's availability for personal counsel be made known? What business groups can the pastor join? And, of course, as the pastor plans sermons and worship services, there needs to be a concerted attempt to understand the concerns of members of the community and address those concerns in preaching and worship.

In His Service,
Your Colleague

Thinking About It—

How would you describe your relationship with your community? How do they view you as a pastor?

Share with some others the most significant ways in which you've been able to minister to your community?

What do you consider to be the three most pressing needs of your community?

21

Loving and Letting Go

DEAR PASTOR,

An effective pastor loves the church. That love is not only for the church as a whole, but also specific and particular churches— the church that I am serving now. And that includes also loving the members of the congregation whom we serve, young and old, those who are likable and those who are not, those who are supportive and those who are critics. A healthy pastoral relationship is a love affair, but then the time comes when we must let go of what and who we have come to love so much.

"Letting go" is one of those things that sometimes pushes in on us rather forcefully, and at other times subtly creeps in and makes itself felt. It's like parenting. Gradually children who are totally dependent on us as their parents begin to move away and make some of their own choices. When they were young, we parents made all their decisions, but gradually they began to choose what to wear, which friends to select, which studies to pursue. Increasingly, as a parent, I could only watch, and hope. And then they left home to strike out on their own and home seemed so empty and I realized that I had to let go. Someone has said that good parenting involves giving our children roots and wings. Roots keep them well-nourished and grounded, but wings will take them away on their own journey.

Pastoring involves a similar kind of repeatedly letting go. After four years, I let go of my first pastorate and moved to the second. I always thought that moving to a new pastorate would be an exciting adventure. It is, but it also involves the pain of saying goodbye to people we have learned to love and have cared for. The people to whom you are going do not understand what you left behind, nor can those you left behind understand the excitement of beginning a new ministry. Some years later I moved to my third pastorate, and then the fourth. Each time we grieved. We said goodbye to dear friends, we shed tears, we looked back, and we felt empty for a while.

And during each pastorate there were members who moved to another congregation and we had to let them go. Some were moving to another community because of a job transfer and some were moving to a neighboring congregation which apparently attracted them more. A couple of times a whole group left at once to form another congregation. Such splintering brings a special kind of pain and needs to be handled wisely. Sometimes we did handle it wisely; sometimes we didn't. It was painful. But nobody had warned me about this.

And then there are the deaths within a congregation. Whether young or old, expected or sudden, the tearing away brings a unique kind of pain. And the more you were attached to such a person, the deeper is the hurt. A long-tenured colleague of mine said that during the first seven years of a pastorate, a funeral is a time when you bury a parishioner. The second seven years you find you are burying a friend. After more years than that you feel like you're burying a family member. Each step brings deeper grief. It's good to remember that at a time when pastoral tenures are getting longer.

But while I write all this, I have become increasingly conscious of the greatest letting go that occurs among us on a regular basis. We are sinful; we sin daily; intentionally and unintentionally. In the process we accumulate for ourselves guilt before the holiness of our great God. And I have had the privilege of standing before the special, beloved, yet sinful people of God every Sunday morning and promise them that on the basis of the grace of God and the finished work of Jesus Christ, God has let go of their sin and guilt. What can possibly be more powerful, richer, and more eternally valuable than that?! I have always resisted the movement in a lot of liturgies today to downplay the assurance of pardon and I've insisted that I do not pardon or absolve, but I can give the assurance of God's grace that pardons on the basis of his word. What a privilege! But at the same time, what a privilege to remind parishioners who are burdened because they seem unable to forgive themselves of some failure that it's OK to let go of it. God does and they may too.

And then, on the human side, there is the biggest step of all—retirement. When we retire we not only let go of a full schedule and the weariness we are feeling, but of special relationships with dear friends, and of a pastorate that has defined us for so long. We let go of so much we begin to wonder who we are. I was surprised to find how hard it became. It feels like we have left our identity behind.

Most thinking today reminds a retiring pastor that a move should be made to another congregation. Find a whole new church home, they say. Maybe so. But those who quickly suggest this, fail to realize how painful such a move can be. The members of the congregation the pastor has served, perhaps for many years, have become like family and to leave them makes the degree of pain even higher.

When I reached that point, I realized that much of my life so far has been marked by acquiring, achieving, getting, and holding on to things. It's not that I was a person driven to get ahead financially and or to acquire a lot of this world's goods. I worked hard to get an excellent education with good degrees, all the way to a DMin. And along the way I was able to acquire a fair amount of material success, with a lot of good things, nice vacations, and a comfortable home, a pretty pleasant standard of living, and adequate funds for the latter years. We have invested ourselves thoroughly to have children who are a credit to us, respected in the community, serving well in all kinds of various kingdom causes with families that are a joy. I have worked hard to achieve a sense of accomplishment in the ministry, so that when I retired in 2002, I felt I could look back on forty years of very good ministry. To be sure there were down times and weaknesses, and I'm all too well-aware of my failures and weaknesses in ministry. But I have been able to serve four excellent congregations in very satisfactory ways and leave behind me a record of very good ministerial accomplishments. It's significant that I was given a position at the seminary as an experienced pastor. And through it all I have surely accumulated a lot of status—as a family, a Christian man, a pastor, a churchman, and a number of other ways. I do not aim to be vain or proud. I am very surprised at this and find myself thinking often, "Look at all that God did with little Howie from Muskegon!"

But now I am in the chapter of life when much of it is reversing. Instead of accumulating and achieving, I am letting go. I've had to let go of the pastorate and the role of being a pastor. The four congregations I served were always considered in my heart as "my churches." I know they were Christ's but they were entrusted to me to influence, form, shape, guide and shepherd. Especially during the twenty-four years of Hillcrest I shaped it more than I ever realized. But no more. I have no influence on the life of the congregations I served. I can only watch. Whether I like what is happening, or not, I have had to let go of the possibility of any influence over the course of their events any more. Sometimes that is very freeing, but sometimes I am very saddened by that.

I've had to let go of my status in the church too. Oh, I still have some among those who are my peers, and I still "work at the seminary," but most people today don't recall that I was a successful pastor, a pretty good preacher, officer of synod five times, and someone who had a hand in shaping a number of denominational issues. To some it's "Vanderwell who?" I'm reminded of that every time I happen to tell a class about the ministry of Rev. P. Eldersveld, and his influence through the Back to God Hour, and none of them even know who he was . . . and I think, "Yes, I have that coming pretty soon too."

Some of that sense of loss is natural, and goes pretty well. Some of it is welcome and I am grateful to do so. Other parts of it are involuntary, even forced, and causes grieving, and some pain. I know this process will continue until I finally have to let go of everything in this life, leave it all behind, and enter my eternal home in heaven. I remember clearly the day when my father was nearing the end of his life on earth. My parents' medical expenses had pretty well depleted all they had accumulated at one point. With some sadness, Dad told me that when the day of his death finally arrives he will be leaving this life much like he was when he came here as an immigrant boy. "I came to American virtually penniless," he said, "and it looks like I will be that way at the end too. It has all gone full cycle." There is something very sad, but poignant, about that. Let me identify a few of the areas in which this letting-go process is taking place, either visibly or invisibly, sometimes voluntarily and sometimes forced.

I have come to realize that there is such a thing as letting go healthily. I must aim for that, and prepare for that. Not all acts of letting go are so healthy. I have seen some that are poorly done, counterproductive, even mean-spirited, and leaving a number of matters unfinished. A healthy letting go, on the other hand, generally involves several ingredients. First, there is intentional *acceptance*. It must and will happen. We cannot avoid such experiences, and it's best that we are not caught by surprise. When we accept the reality of such experiences, we are in a better position to prepare for them. Second, we must acknowledge *unfinished work*. Each time I have left a pastorate, I have been conscious of the fact that there are many good folks with whom I wish I had spent much more time. "What a shame," I would tell myself, "that I didn't spent more time listening to their story and sharing their friendship instead of working so hard." And I would look at the life of the congregation and wish that I had addressed certain needs more effectively. I never felt free to mouth the words "my work is done here." I know it's never done and never will be. Then I must also put forth some effort to *mend brokenness*. Unfortunately, such things happen in the pastorate. Feelings are hurt, wounds occur, scars are left, and harsh words have been spoken and never healed over. Just as it is necessary for a family to effect some reconciliation before a loved one passes away, so at times a pastor and congregation need some reconciliation before moving on. It may involve private apologies or public acknowledgements, but both are better than allowing things to simmer. There will also be times of *celebrating accomplishments*. True, some of the accomplishments in the pastorate are invisible and internal, but it can be healthy for all to note the specific ways in which the Lord's blessing has been poured out during a certain period of ministry. Be careful, however, that the intent is not to praise ourselves, but to properly acknowledge that God deserves praise for all fruit that ripens. And those of us who leave and let go, must also understand that we are obligated to contribute some efforts that will serve the cause of *continuity in ministry* after we have left. When one pastor leaves, preparations are made for a new pastor to arrive. Though this may take some time, the pastor who leaves can serve the transition well by leaving enough of the nonconfidential records, reports and studies that will be helpful to the next pastor. And, finally, when we let go, we must always *treasure the memories*. A pastoral ministry is a highly intense life of deep relationships which involve precious memories. Good memories of living and growing together are to be kept forever. I personally cherish a huge storehouse of memories that I have accumulated through the years of my ministry. I hope I never lose them.

Much of this came into focus in 2016 when the March issue of the *Banner*, a church periodical, carried an article by Robert Ritzema, who was reflecting on his own experience of aging. He said the aging process involves both "loss" and "simplification." I found it helpful when he articulated both of those. I've been reflecting here on the first one—letting go.

But Ritzema went on to claim that "simplification" is another factor in this aging process. I wasn't so conscious of that, but with some thought it became clear. My commitments, duties, and responsibilities are much more simplified. My "to do" list is shorter; I end the day not with frustration that I didn't get enough done, but with the satisfaction that I accomplished about what I hoped to. My list of phone calls to make is very short, and few calls come in for me anymore. As a matter of fact, I don't even answer the phone very much anymore. I leave that to my wife. My schedule is simpler, and my calendar doesn't have nearly as much written on it. And yet I'm rarely bored; I feel active all the time. Which means I have been able to manage selectively what I am involved in, whereas before retirement I didn't manage it all, it managed me. So today I juggle just a few balls compared to the dozen or more balls I juggled when active in the ministry. Even my preaching schedule is much simpler. I don't have to have six sermons rolling around in my brain for the next few weeks.

But it seems to me there is one stage in-between the poles of loss and simplification that Ritzema missed in that *Banner* article. Loss and simplification need "cherish" between them. He suggested that numerous losses involve some grieving activity and that's OK. I surely can sense that. I've done my share of grieving and for that matter I still do. I feel the pain of my lost pastoral identity, and of Hillcrest, and of the greater and higher level of strength and energy. So I'm usually pretty aware of a thread of sadness that runs through my consciousness. It was, of course, most severe during the early months of retirement. But it continues from time to time. Giving ourselves the right to feel that pain is a healthy part of it.

But the word "cherish" is another one that I'd put in there, as a word and as a healthy discipline. I view "cherish" as a warm and tender word, one which points to the pleasant and grateful emotions associated with the activity of taking memories of things past and tenderly turning them around in our heart, like a precious stone, vowing not to take them for granted. I do a lot of cherishing. I cherish the years of my life—nearly eight decades is a long time, beyond normal life expectancy, defying what three bouts with cancer tried to do. The years have been many and their quality has been superb. I also cherish my family. I've been blessed with a rich and steady marriage to a wonderful woman who's been a great companion, faithful support in ministry, an excellent mother to our children and grandchildren, and one who is understanding of who I am and what makes me tick. She even has supportively entered the kind of retirement that we've fashioned for ourselves.

I also cherish the four pastorates I've been privileged to serve. My identity will forever be associated with Lebanon, Trinity, Bethel and Hillcrest. Those four were very different in both their joys and challenges, but they were all good places to serve, congregations who did indeed thrive under my ministry, grew in faithfulness, and responded to us with love and support. They were the kind of which many pastors would be envious. I cherish them each. I also cherish the way in which God has helped us through trials and sicknesses. When we married, I never entertained the notion that Ellie and I might lose a child at birth, or that I would have these encounters with cancer, or that Ellie would have all her joint replacements, or have to deal with the post-polio problems she has. At the beginning we would dream about life being nice and smooth, but it turned out to be up-and-down, rough-and-tumble at times. But you know what? Through all of that it proved to be rich and full to the degree we never expected. So I cherish how God has turned our sorrows into joys, and our difficulties in riches. And as I think about all of that, I'm conscious of the fact that I cherish so many wonderful people whom God has brought into our lives for companionship, encouragement, friendship, and support. In each of our difficulties there were special people who pulled up alongside and blessed us; in each pastorate there were key people who made such a difference; and in each chapter of ministry I have been able to serve with others who were top-notch. And I consider each of them to be a gift from God to me.

So as I review the process of growing older, and the chapter of retirement, and look carefully in that rearview mirror, I see there have been losses and I grieve them; there have been serendipities from God and I cherish them; and life has become more simplified and I welcome that.

These stages may seem so far ahead of you now that you can barely imagine them. They will arrive sooner than you think, and even now you may be able to recognize some of the faint beginnings of each stage.

It all is a foreshadowing of that final day when we have to let everything go and enter the final stage of our journey where we can take nothing along except memories and the fruit that the Savior has harvested. When the journey is finished, memories and fruit will remain with us.

As I write these thoughts I recall a conversation I had with my doctor one day while in his office. We were comparing our professions, and he, a devout Christian man, expressed envy of my role as a pastor. When I questioned him on that, his reply was, "Sooner or later, I will lose all my patients; you will keep all yours forever!"

I'll never let go of that!

In His Service,
Your Colleague

Thinking About It—

> What memories or reflections come to mind for you when we talk about "letting go"?
>
> In what ways does the pastoral ministry thrust us into "letting go" experiences.

Suggestions for further reading

Barnes, M. Craig. *The Pastor as Minor Poet*. Eerdmans, 2009. From his wide and wise experience, Barnes offers insights into the text and subtext of the pastoral life.

Bass, Dorothy C. *Receiving the Day: Christian Practices for Opening the Gift of Time*. Jossey-Bass, 2000. Keeping Sabbath and managing the gift of time is an essential discipline for any Christian leader.

Bolsinger, Tod E. *It Takes a Church to Raise a Christian: How the Community of God Transforms Lives*. Brazos, 2004. Bolsinger critiques American individualism and claims that a relationship-centered, sacramental life will transform worship and witness.

Dawn, Marva J. *A Royal "Waste" of Time: The Splendor of Worshiping God and Being Church for the World*. Eerdmans, 1999. Since worship is at the heart of a church, a church leader and pastor will do well to cultivate the art of worship healthily.

DeKruyter, Arthur H., with Quentin J. Schultze. *The Suburban Church: Practical Advice for Authentic Ministry*. Westminster John Knox, 2008. From his highly successful ministry at Christ Church Oak Brook, DeKruyter offers helpful reflections on how to meaningfully minister to a suburban congregation.

Hauerwas, Stanley, and William H. Willimon. *Resident Aliens: Life in the Christian Colony*. Abingdon, 1989. Here is a provocative Christian assessment of culture and ministry for people who know that something is wrong.

London, H. B., Jr., and Neil B. Wiseman. *They Call Me Pastor: How to Love the Ones you Lead*. Regal, 2000. Both London and Wiseman draw on their ministry experiences to give insights into the role of a shepherd, counselor, and leader who loves those being led.

Peterson, Eugene H. *A Long Obedience in the Same Direction.* InterVarsity, 2000. Peterson offers reflections on the Psalms, which provide rich insight into discipleship in an instant society.

Peterson, Eugene H. *The Pastor: A Memoir.* HarperOne, 2011. Peterson, the translator of *The Message,* offers his insights into a lifetime of ministry in the pastorate.

Smedes, Lewis B. *How Can It Be All Right When Everything Is All Wrong?* Harper & Row, 1982. Real believing is done with our deepest self when we know in the deep places of our soul that it is all right even when our heart tells us everything is all wrong.

Webber, Robert E. *Worship Is a Verb.* Word, 1985. This is Webber's basic book on the theology of worship. It provides excellent foundational material. Supplementary books by the same author will also serve well.

Yancey, Philip. *The Question That Never Goes Away: Why?* Zondervan, 2013. As a sequel to some of his other books, Yancey gives us permission to doubt, yet never abandon faith.